O9-BTN-953

A Day in the Life of Hawaii extends special thanks and appreciation to the following for their help and cooperation in making this project possible.

FIRST HAWAIIAN BANK

Duty Free Shoppers

Matson

HAWAIIAN TELEPHONE GTE

PRI Pacific Resources, Inc. Hawaii's Energy Company

The Hawaii Visitors Bureau

Department of Planning and Economic Development

UNITED AIRLINES

Sheraton Hotels in Hawaii

SONY Broadcast

Kazuyoshi Nomachi

The book you are holding in your hands is a moment frozen in time, an impression of Hawaii taken on Friday, December 2, 1983, by fifty of the world's leading photographers. No picture here is more than twenty-four hours older or younger than any other, and no picture here has been shot for any purpose other than to document the harmonies and paradoxes of life in Hawaii as it was lived on this one day.

The photographers were stationed in places and situations where we guessed and hoped that their pictures might best reflect the texture of the day—in both its ordinariness and individuality. One such place was the ranch country on the Big Island, another was the delivery room of a hospital on Oahu. One photographer greeted dawn with a group of tuna fishermen, another covered a local beauty pageant rehearsal that evening. Yet wherever cameras were clicking, the unplanned, the unexpected, even the unseen found their way into the frame.

This year, Hawaii's heterogeneous people celebrate twenty-five years of statehood, years that have seen the full blooming of a proud modern society. This society has grown up in one of the loveliest climates and settings known to man. This is affirmed by the four million visitors who pass through Hawaii each year.

A Day in the Life of Hawaii does not claim to be the true record of even one day. A day cannot be collected as it passes by in a blaze of light between shadows. December 2 in Hawaii yielded its quirky, constant secrets more subtly. There are several hundred photographs here, culled from more than 60,000. But even 60,000 images barely hint at the infinite moments that passed through the beaches and hills and homes and hearts of Hawaii on that day. *A Day in the Life of Hawaii* belongs to them—to each smile, each silence, each crashing wave saved only in memory.

Michael Shayegani

Sam Garcia

Library of Congress Cataloging in Publication Data
Main entry under title:

A Day in the life of Hawaii.

Includes index.
1. Hawaii—Description and travel—1981—Views.
2. Hawaii—Anniversaries, etc.—Pictorial works. I. Smolan, Rick.
II. Cohen, David, 1955-
DU621.5.D38 1984
996.9'04 84-7224
ISBN 0-89480-760-9

Project Directors
Rick Smolan and David Cohen

Art Director
Leslie Smolan

Cover Photography
Dan Dry

Workman Publishing Company
1 West 39 Street
New York, New York 10018

Printed in Japan
First printing August 1984

10 9 8 7 6 5 4 3

Photographed by 50 of the world's leading photojournalists on December 2, 1983

Workman Publishing, New York

Terry Ferrante

A Day In The Life Of Hawaii

737 BISHOP STREET SUITE 2860 HONOLULU, HI 96813 (808) 922-0571

November 5, 1983

Dear Photographer,

I'm writing to invite you to work on a project that my partner, David Cohen, and I are in the process of organizing here in Hawaii. I'm an American freelance photographer and for the past ten years I've been working on assignments around the world for many magazines including Time, Newsweek, Fortune, and National Geographic.

In 1984, Hawaii will be celebrating it's 25th anniversary of statehood. Our idea is to create a special book for this Silver Jubilee celebration. To do this, we want to position fifty of the world's best photographers throughout the Hawaiian islands and to give each photographer the same 24-hour period to capture a typical Hawaiian day on film. The result of this 24-hour shoot will be a hardcover book to be titled "A Day in the Life of Hawaii" (DITLOHA for short).

Here's the deal. On Friday December 2, 1983 you will be asked to photograph a specific aspect of Hawaiian life. The aim of this project is not to make the definitive statement about Hawaii. Nor is the intention to concentrate on the rich, the famous or the powerful. Instead, you will be asked to apply your photographic skills to something even more challenging: to make extraordinary photographs of ordinary events.

We will be giving each of you a specific assignment, but you will also have the freedom to shoot whatever you discover by accident on the day - the assignment is just a starting point. All we ask is that you make great pictures.

If all goes well, the project will produce a large format hardcover book, a one-hour television documentary, a calendar featuring the best photographs from the project and a travelling exhibit of photographic prints. DITLOHA will also involve a statewide photography contest.

Although this project has the personal support of the governor, the Hawaiian Visitor's Bureau, and a number of private companies, it is <u>not</u> a public relations exercise or a tourist promotion. Everyone supporting the project understands that you are journalists and they will have no editorial control over what you shoot or what ends up in the book. DITLOHA will be an honest look at Hawaii, not just another book of pretty Hawaiian picture postcards.

By the same token there is no guarantee that every photographer will get a picture in the book. That depends on whether you have a good day on December 2nd.

At the moment, the eight of us on staff are frantically putting the last pieces in place to make sure everything goes smoothly when you and the other photographers arrive. If working with us on this crazy idea appeals to you, here are a few things you need to know and few things we need from you very quickly:

1) Biography: Don't be modest. We need as much information about your photography career as possible - awards, exhibits, books published, major magazine stories, etc. We would also appreciate a good photo of you - in action if possible.

2) Film: Eastman Kodak will be using this project to test their new professional Kodachrome films. We will supply you with 30 rolls of film (Kodachrome, Ektachrome or Tri-X). It would help us to know your requirements in advance.

3) Ground Transportation: If your assignment requires it, you will be provided with a rental car courtesy of Holiday rent-a-car.

4) Insurance: Although we have liability insurance for everyone working on the project (i.e. if you drop your camera on the mayor's daughter's head, we are covered), we will not be able to insure you personally (i.e. if you fall into an active volcano, you are not covered). You must have your own insurance.

5) Room mates: If you take advantage of the hotel rooms provided to you courtesy of Sheraton Hotels during your eight days in Oahu, you will share a twin room with a famous photographer at absolutely no extra charge.

6) Payment: All expenses including air and ground travel, meals and accomodations will be covered by us. You will be paid an honorarium of $350 for the day's shooting. In addition you will receive an $800 Radio Shack Model 100 lap portable computer and a free membership in the PHOTO-1 Network (a communications network for professional photographers).

We will be sending out more information to each photographer in the next few days but in the meantime, this letter is to ask if the idea interests you and if you will be able to join us. We hope you can make it.

Best regards,

Rick Smolan

Rick Smolan

• *Previous pages 4–5*
5:45 AM on the island of Molokai. James Kelii Mawae, a housepainter, and Ernest Puoi, a farmer, share an hour of fishing and friendship.
Photographer:
Michael Shayegani

• *Previous pages 6–7*
The glamour of the Pacific silhouettes horseman Gilbert Medieros after an early morning cattle drive at South Point, the southernmost spot in the United States.
Photographer:
Sam Garcia

• *Left*
A small crew from the tuna boat "Orion" catches bait in the shallow waters off Maui.
Photographer:
Stephanie Maze

• *Above*
Nearby, a U.S. Navy submarine surfaces in time to catch the first morning sun.
Photographer:
David Doubilet

King Street
Kapiolani Blvd
EXIT ONLY
King St.

• *Left*

Morning traffic streams toward downtown Honolulu on *Interstate* H-1. The humor of the name pales at rush hour, when Honolulu overwhelms its antiquated road system.

Photographer:
Rick Smolan

• *Above*

Sixteen-month-old Asia Lueras, still asleep in the living room of her parents' old wood-and-stone house in Manoa, one of the cooler residential valleys that climb into the hills behind Honolulu.

Photographer:
Leonard Lueras

• *Below*

Air-assault trainees receive a safety lecture at Schofield Barracks, home of the 25th Infantry Division and the largest of eight Army posts in Hawaii.

Photographer:
Alon Reininger

• *Right*

An early morning jog stirs the main quadrangle at Schofield Barracks.

Photographer:
Alon Reininger

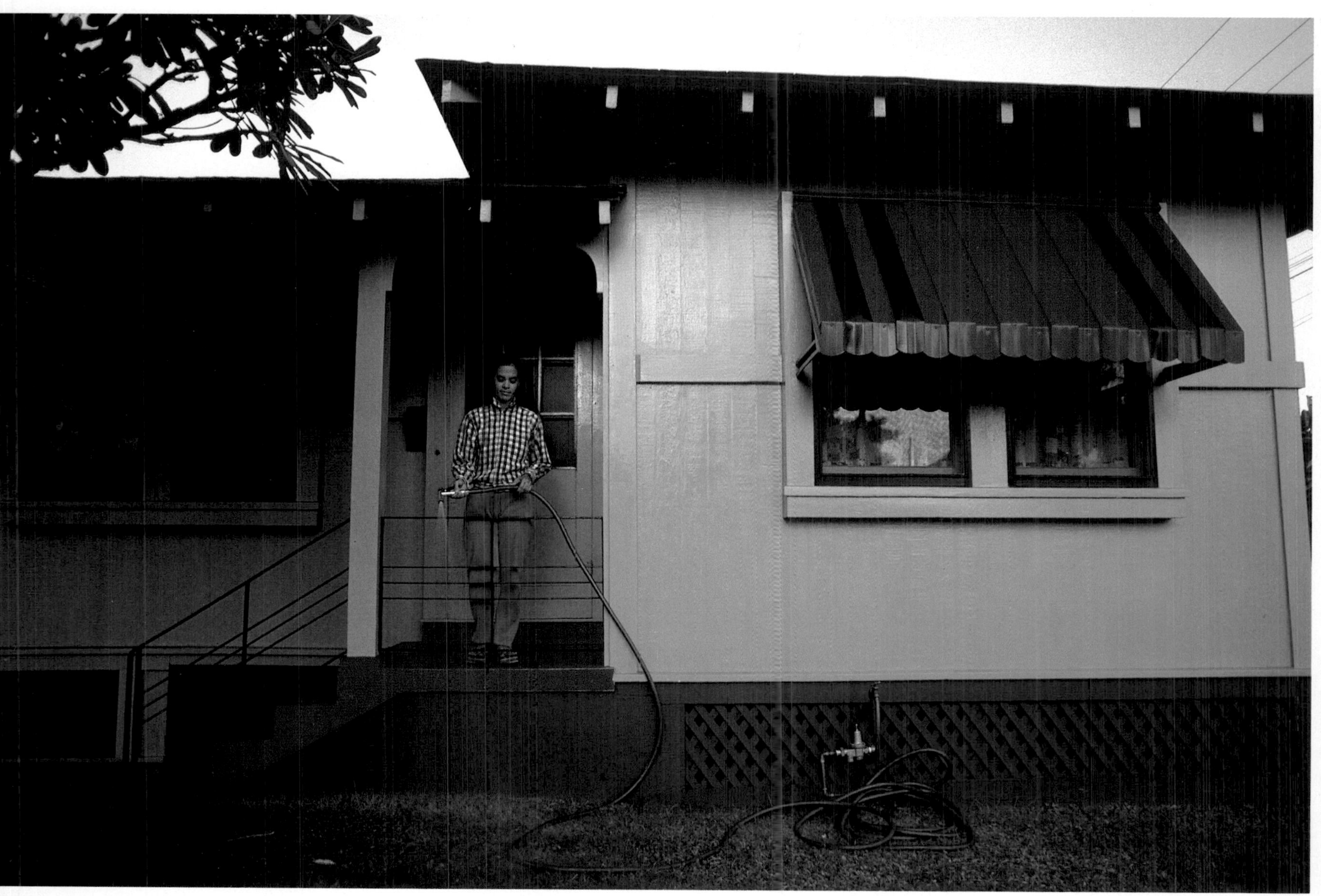

• *Left*

Elias Fernandez, known as "Pantaloon," with his prize fighting cock. As old as the century, Pantaloon came to the island of Kauai from the Philippines in 1927 to work on a sugar plantation.

Photographer:
Kent Kobersteen

• *Above*

958 Sixth Avenue in Kaimuki, a quiet middle-class district of Honolulu.

Photographer:
Leonard Lueras

• *Following pages 18–19*

With a yank on his bamboo pole, a Maui fisherman lands a tuna, or ahi, aboard the "Orion." The bait thrower, far left, tosses fresh bait to attract the tuna while water jets simulate a teeming school of fish. Once the tuna are lured into a feeding frenzy, they are easily hooked. Fifteen such boats haul about 50 percent of the state's annual catch.

Photographer:
Stephanie Maze

• *Following pages 20–21*

At the 500-acre J. J. Ackerman Ranch in Kealakekua, Hawaii, three-year-old Dodge Ackerman gets a scolding from his mother, Noel.

Photographer:
Star Black

Stephanie Maze

Star Black

John Loengard

Previous page

Taro patch, Waipio Valley, the Big Island.

Photographer:
John Loengard

Below, left

Wilfred and Violet Nonaka own and operate Honolulu's Alex Drive-In, a busy burgers-and-fries hangout since 1958.

Photographer:
P. F. Bentley

Below, right

Tandem surfing experts Kathy Terada and John DeSoto warm up at Makaha Beach.

Photographer:
Arthur Grace

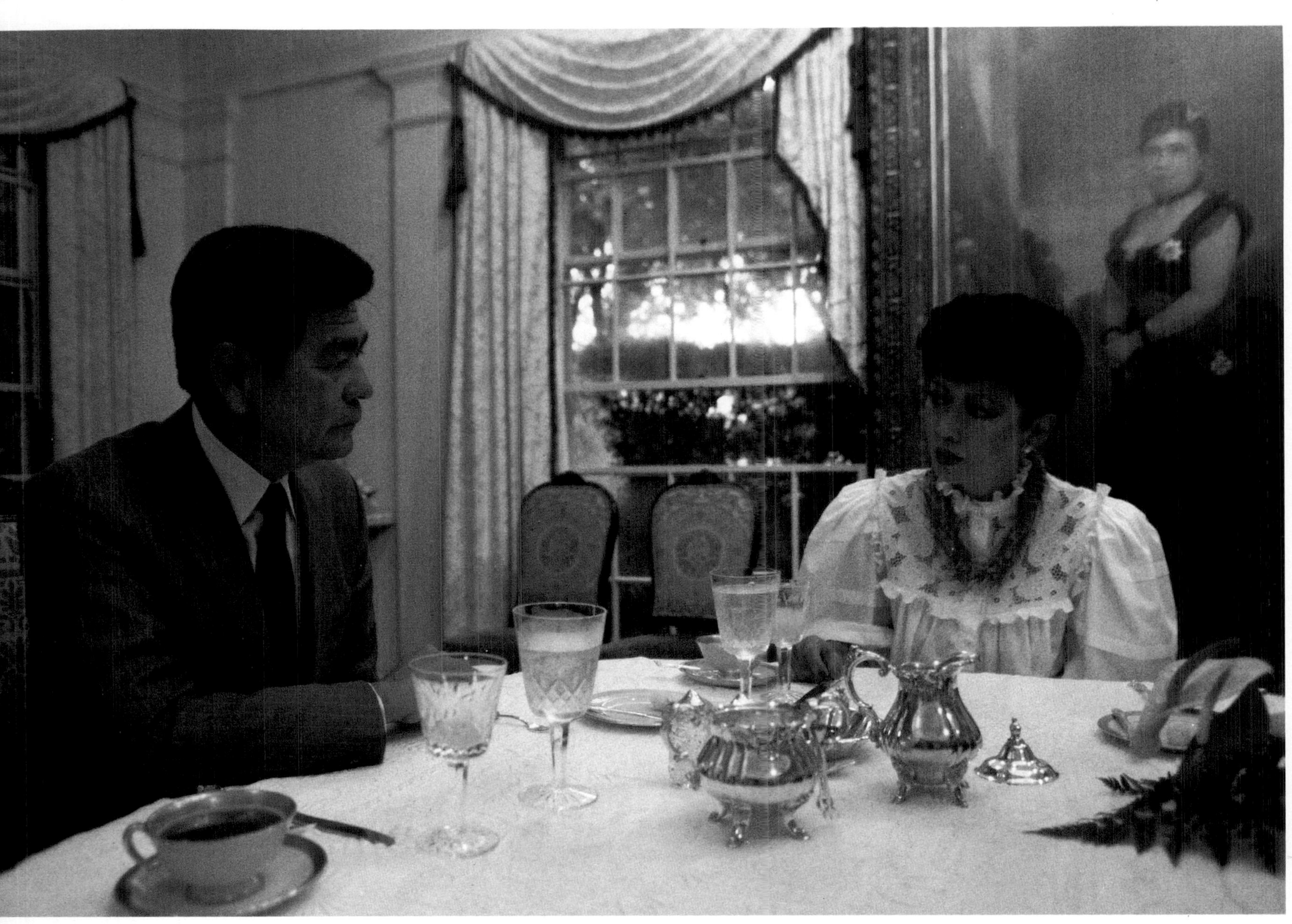

• *Left*

A portrait of Princess Kaiulani (1875–1899) commands a quiet corner of the bustling 1200-room Sheraton Princess Kaiulani Hotel in Waikiki. The hotel is built on the site of Ainahau, the estate where the reclusive princess, educated in England, spent most of her brief life among tame peacocks and loyal advisers.

Photographer:
Gerd Ludwig

• *Above*

Governor and Mrs. George Ariyoshi eating breakfast at Washington Place, the official governor's residence in downtown Honolulu. Behind Jean Ariyoshi, an 1892 portrait of Queen Liliuokalani, Hawaii's last reigning monarch and a former owner of the mansion.

Photographer:
Michael Evans

• *Following page*

All 822 students, faculty and staff members of Sacred Hearts Academy gather for a portrait after daily Mass. Sacred Hearts is a Catholic girls' school in Honolulu's Kaimuki neighborhood. At one point during the session, photographer P. F. Bentley, perched on a ten-foot ladder, told the girls that if they really took their time getting set up, there wouldn't be any school that day. The crowd went wild.

Photographer:
P. F. Bentley

P.F. Bentley

ACRED · HEARTS ·

8:30 AM

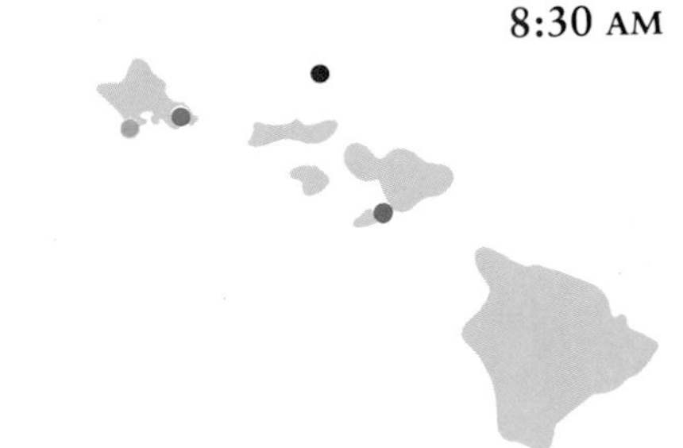

• *Above*

First Hawaiian Bank CEO John Bellinger talks to New York while flying in the bank's jet with Roger MacArthur to a lunchtime appointment with Hannibal Tavares, the mayor of Maui.

Photographer:
Rick Smolan

• *Right*

Honolulu-bound commuter traffic snakes up the pali on Oahu's suburban Windward Side.

Photographer:
Rick Smolan

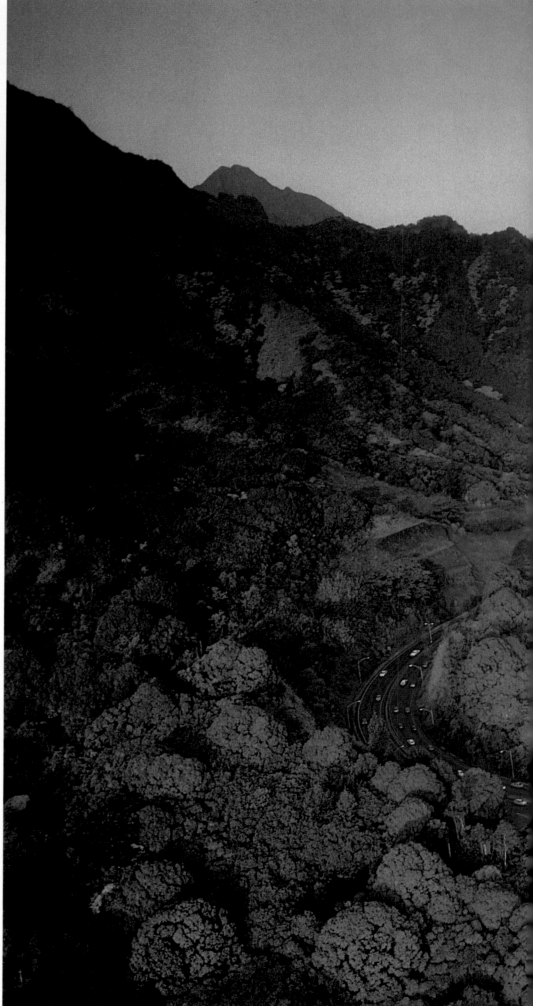

• *Following pages 32–33*

Surface light silhouettes a snorkler 25 feet above lemon butterflyfish and red-shoulder tangs off Molokini Island.

Photographer:
David Doubilet

• *Following pages 34–35*

Shimmering heat rises from a 750°F crude furnace as process operator Paul Mc-Angus checks a pressure gauge at the PRI refinery on Oahu. On December 2 the refinery processed over two million gallons of Alaska North Slope crude for jet fuel, industrial fuel oil, gasoline and diesel fuel. Imported oil supplies more than 90 percent of Hawaii's energy needs at a daily cost of nearly $3 million.

Photographer:
Gregory Heisler

David Doubilet

Gregory Heisler

Eddie Adams

Bob Davis

Previous pages 36–37

The 224,000-acre Parker Ranch on the Big Island, one of the largest ranches in the United States.

Photographer:

Eddie Adams

Previous pages 38–39

Boarding students at Lahainaluna High School, a public school on Maui, grow fruits and vegetables and raise livestock for student consumption. These two boarders are working in the chicken slaughterhouse.

Photographer:

Bob Davis

Below

An irrigation truck waters pineapple fields in the rich Palawai Basin on Lanai, the "Pineapple Isle."

Photographer:

Rich Clarkson

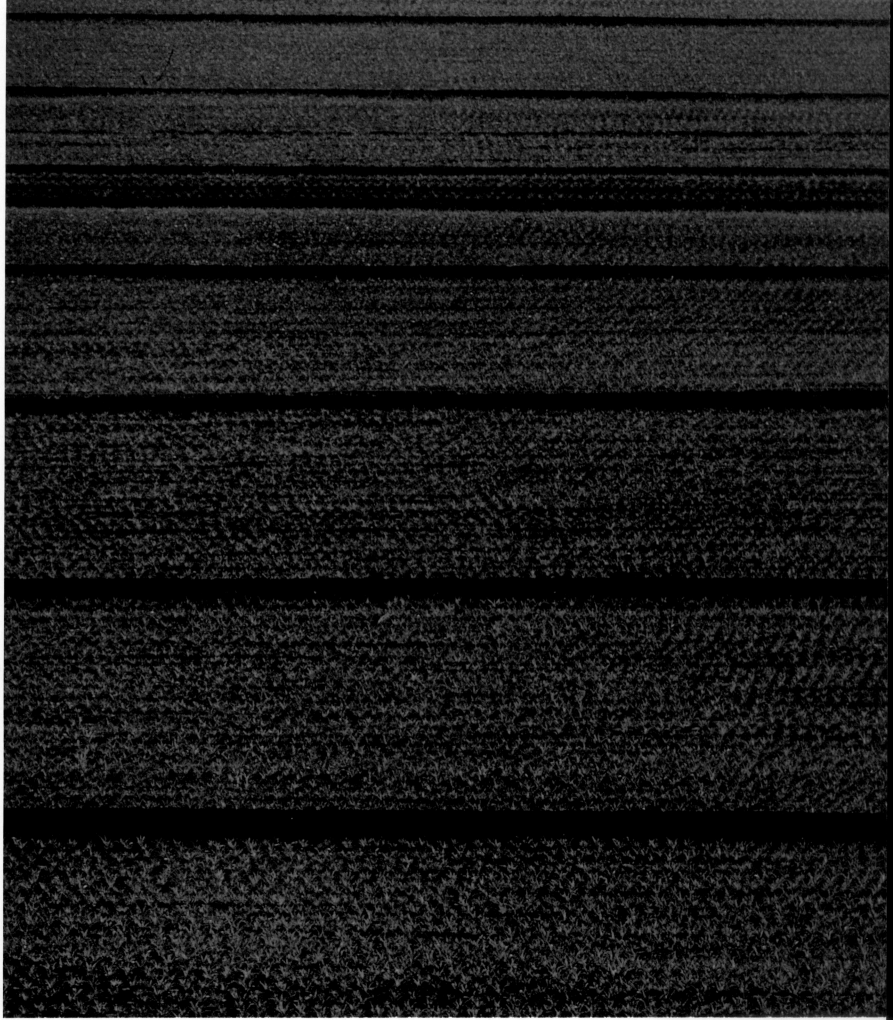

Left
Francisco Mendoza, a cabbage picker on the Big Island.
Photographer:
Mark S. Wexler

9:00 AM

• *Left*

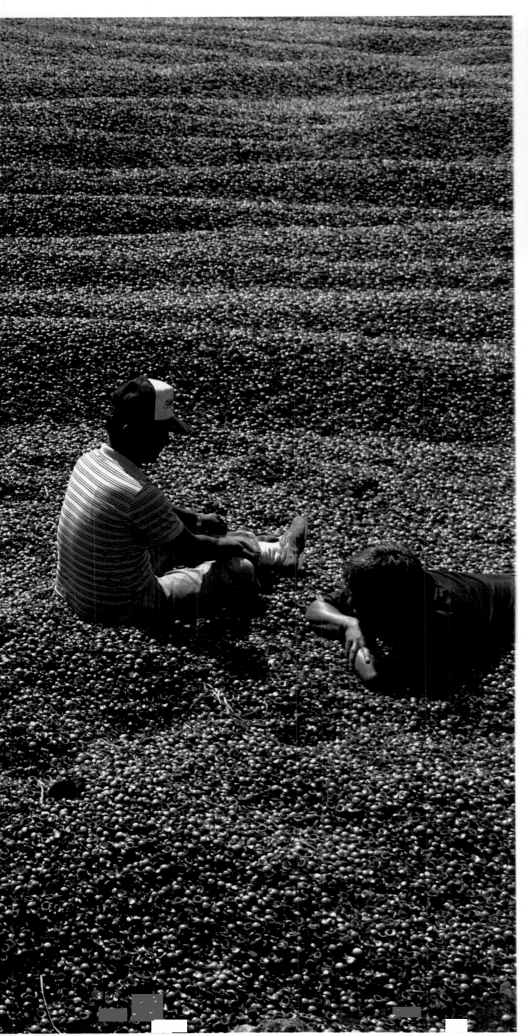

Workers relax on a bed of macadamia nut shells at MacFarms' 2,700-acre plantation on the Big Island.
Photographer:
Diego Goldberg

• *Above*

Inside the MacFarms plant, workers sort the macadamia harvest for shipment to tourist stores in Honolulu and gourmet shops around the world.
Photographer:
Diego Goldberg

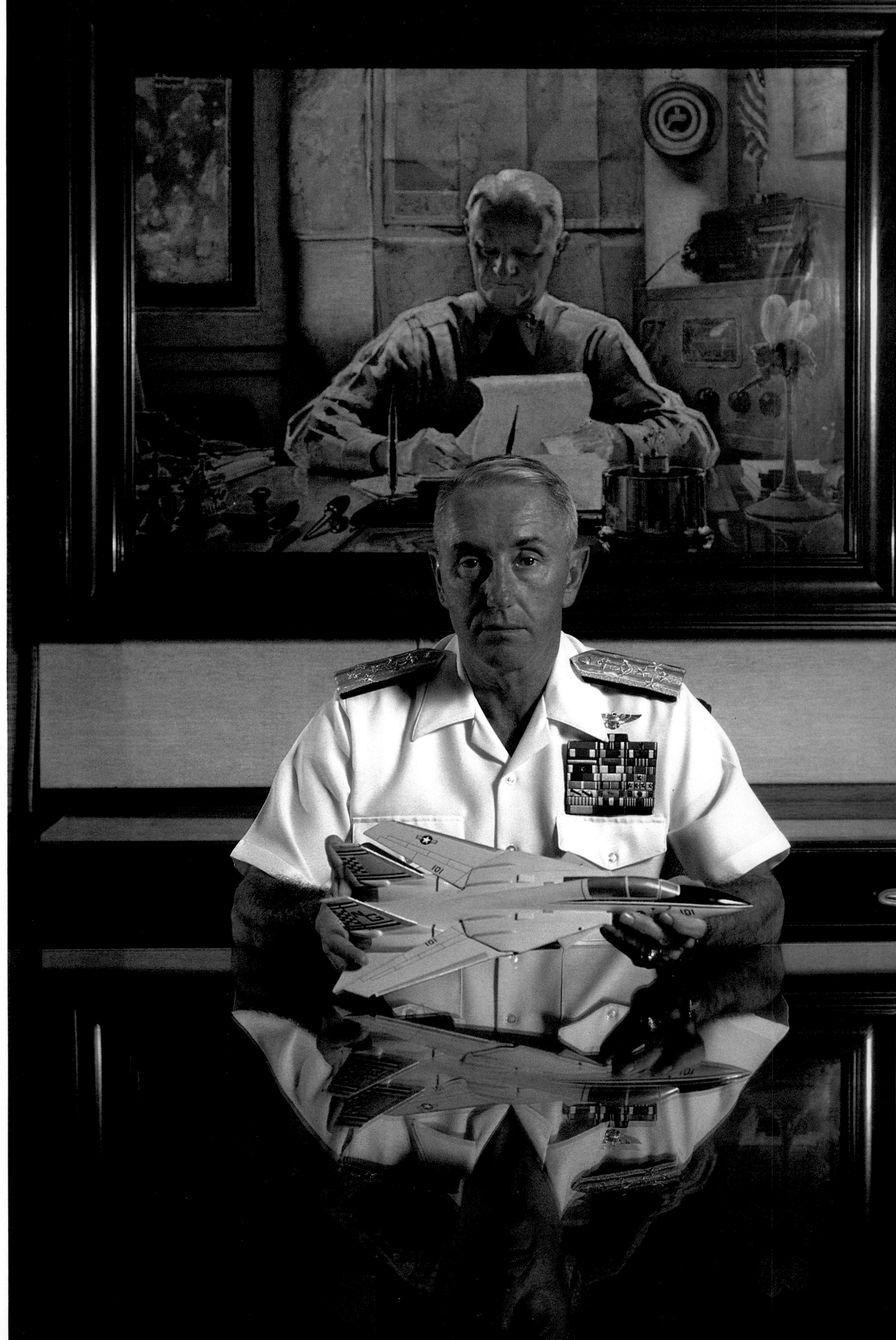

101

Tucked in the crater of a long dormant volcano outside of Honolulu is a tiny community which is home for several thousand soldiers and their families. In some ways, this housing project is like the entire military presence in Hawaii—a vitally important and very powerful part of the state's life and economy that is generally hidden from public view. Raw facts about Hawaii's unobtrusive military establishment are staggering:

- Huge bases and off-base housing sites on Oahu house 125,000 service personnel and their dependents, or about 13 percent of the state's population.

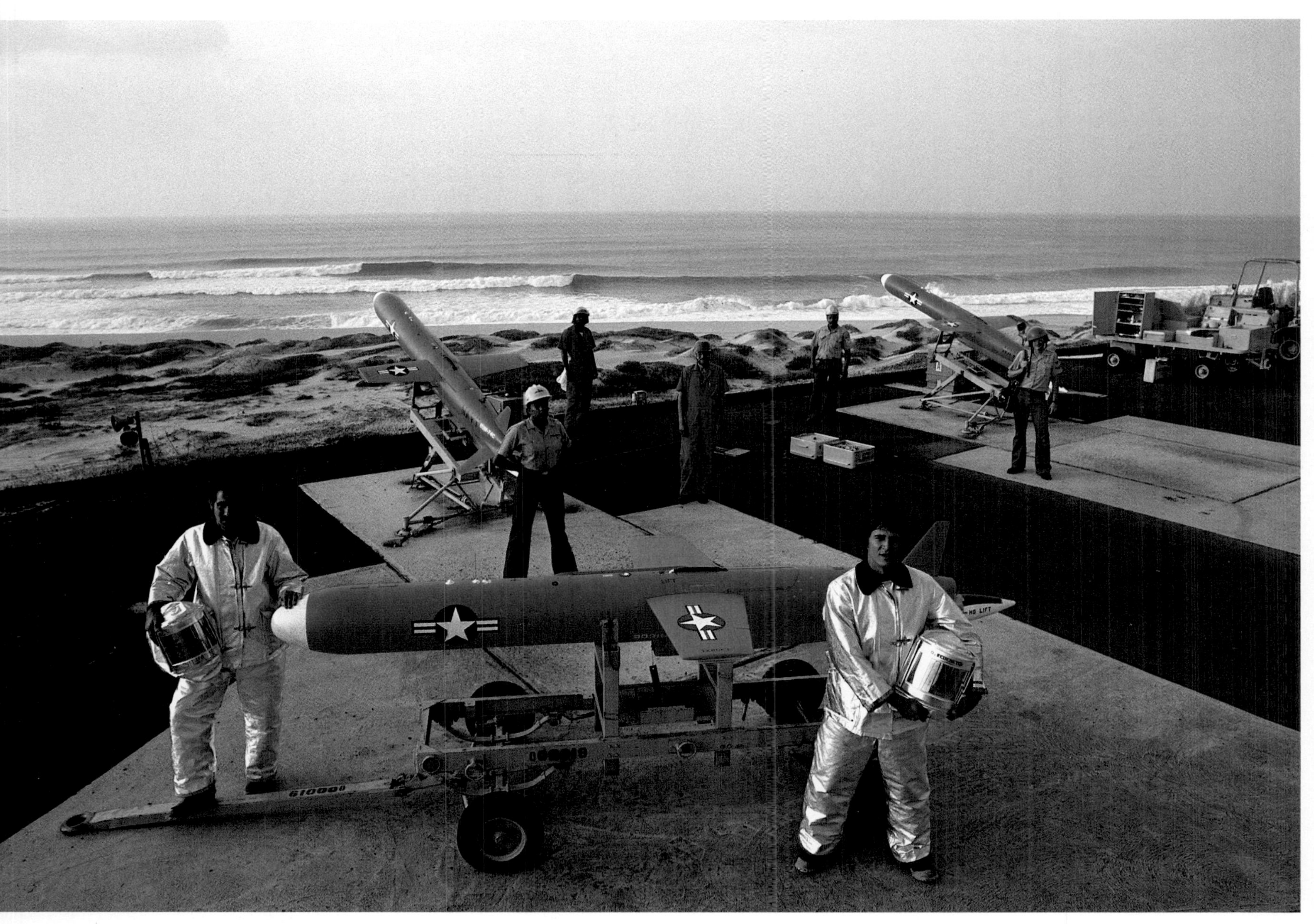

• *Left*
A Norman Rockwell portrait of Admiral Chester Nimitz hangs above Nimitz's original desk at CINCPAC Naval Headquarters, Pearl Harbor. The current occupant of the desk is Commander-in-Chief of the Pacific Fleet, Admiral Sylvester R. Foley, Jr.
Photographer:
Arnaud de Wildenberg

• *Above*
BQM-74C remote-control drones are used for target practice at the Pacific Missile Range, Barking Sands, Kauai.
Photographer:
Frank Salmoiraghi

■ The military employs another 20,000 civilians in technical and administrative jobs, making it Hawaii's largest single employer.
■ In all, the armed services pump $4 million into Hawaii's economy every day, making defense—along with tourism and marijuana—one of the state's largest industries.

From its headquarters in an appropriately unassuming building in Hawaii, the office of the Commander-in-Chief, Pacific (CINCPAC) manages the largest command force in the world, including all American units in the Indian, Arctic and Pacific Oceans.

Five *DITLOHA* photographers—three from Hawaii, one from Israel, and one from France—spent December 2 with the troops.

• *Left*

The 3rd Marine Regiment, 1st Brigade, stands at attention after morning sit-ups at Kaneohe Marine Corps Air Station.

Photographer:
Allan Seiden

• *Above*

At 5:30 AM, the tarmac at Hickam A.F.B. is guarded by Sergeant Granville Noles, Airman First Class John Carpenter and Airman First Class Rod Naico.

Photographer:
Dennis Oda

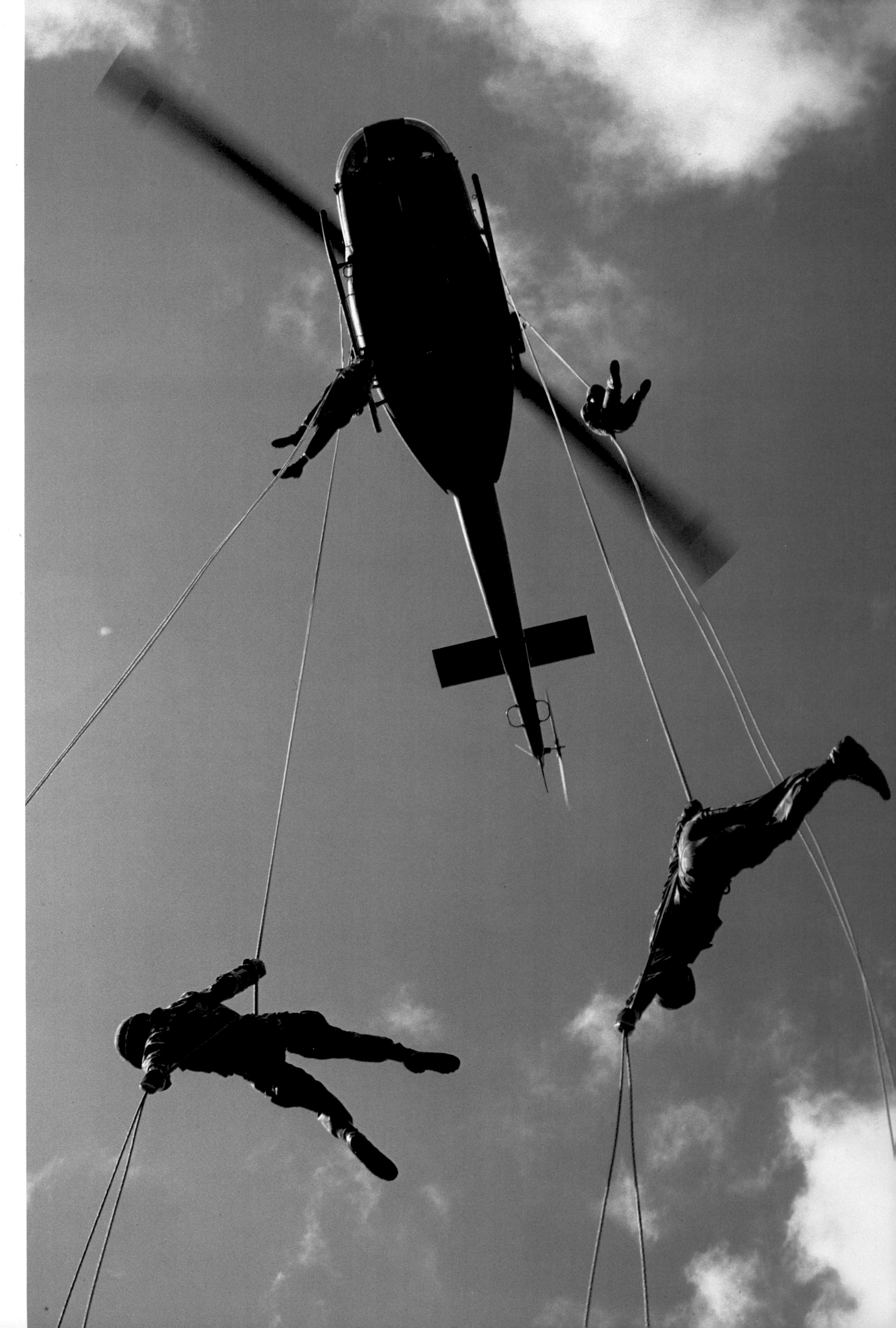

Left

: Army Air Assault School, ainees rappel from a hinook CH-47 helicopter.

otographer:

lon Reininger

• *Left*

A G.I. smile during helicopter-transport exercises at Schofield Barracks.

Photographer:

Alon Reininger

• *Below*

The men of the First Batallion of the 27th Infantry, U.S. Army, practice anti-armor tactics with light weapons and an M60A1 tank.

Photographer:

Alon Reininger

• *Following page*

Local motion on the Waianae coast of Oahu.

Photographer:

Arthur Grace

Arthur Grace

Aaron Chang

Previous page

ccording to top professional urfing photographer Aaron Chang, December 2 rolled in vith the hottest wave action t the Banzai Pipeline in early two years. Chang wam out to the reef with his amera and popped out of he shoulder of this ten-foot vave to grab a shot of Chappy Jennings in the tube.

hotographer:

aron Chang

● *Left*

Ascending from the Molokini reef.

Photographer:

David Doubilet

Above

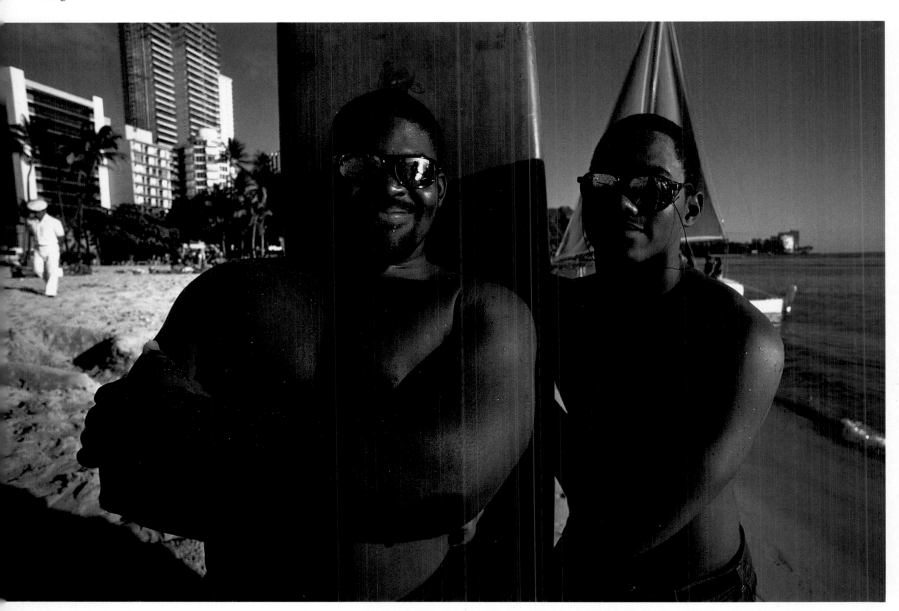

front of the Outrigger otel on Waikiki Beach, embers of the University f Oklahoma football am show off their Big ight muscle. The next day, klahoma's Sooners beat e University of Hawaii ainbows, 21 to 17.

otographer:

erd Ludwig

● *Right*

Over four million people from around the world visit Hawaii during the course of a year, four times the population of the entire state. These visitors have come north from Australia.

Photographer:

Gerd Ludwig

Right

1:34 AM. At Kapiolani/Children's Medical Center in Honolulu, a new day brings a new treasure. Kalala Masalosalo looks at her quiet infant and says, "We're gonna have to come up with a name for you, boy."

The seven-pound, eight-ounce child, later named Ele-Ele, is one of 55 people born in Hawaii on Friday, December 2. Fourteen deaths were also recorded on that day.

Photographer:
Jodi Cobb

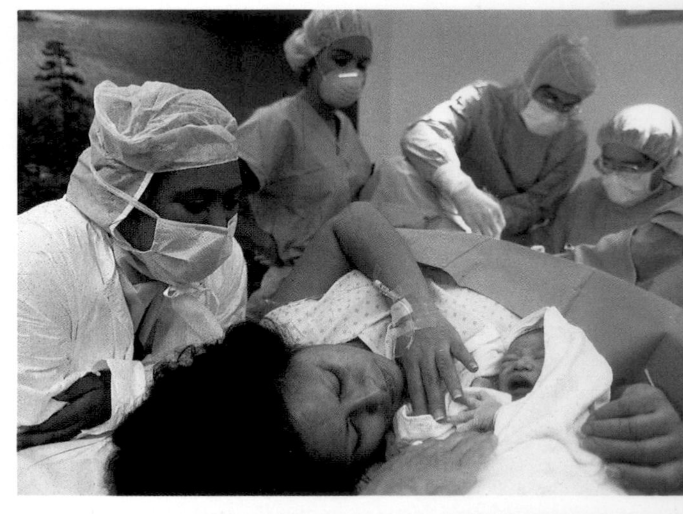

Above

Poipu Beach Park, Kauai.

Photographer:
Sebastiao Salgado

Right

Kaleo Kaina presents his son Frank, born 24 hours earlier.

Photographer:
Michael O'Brien

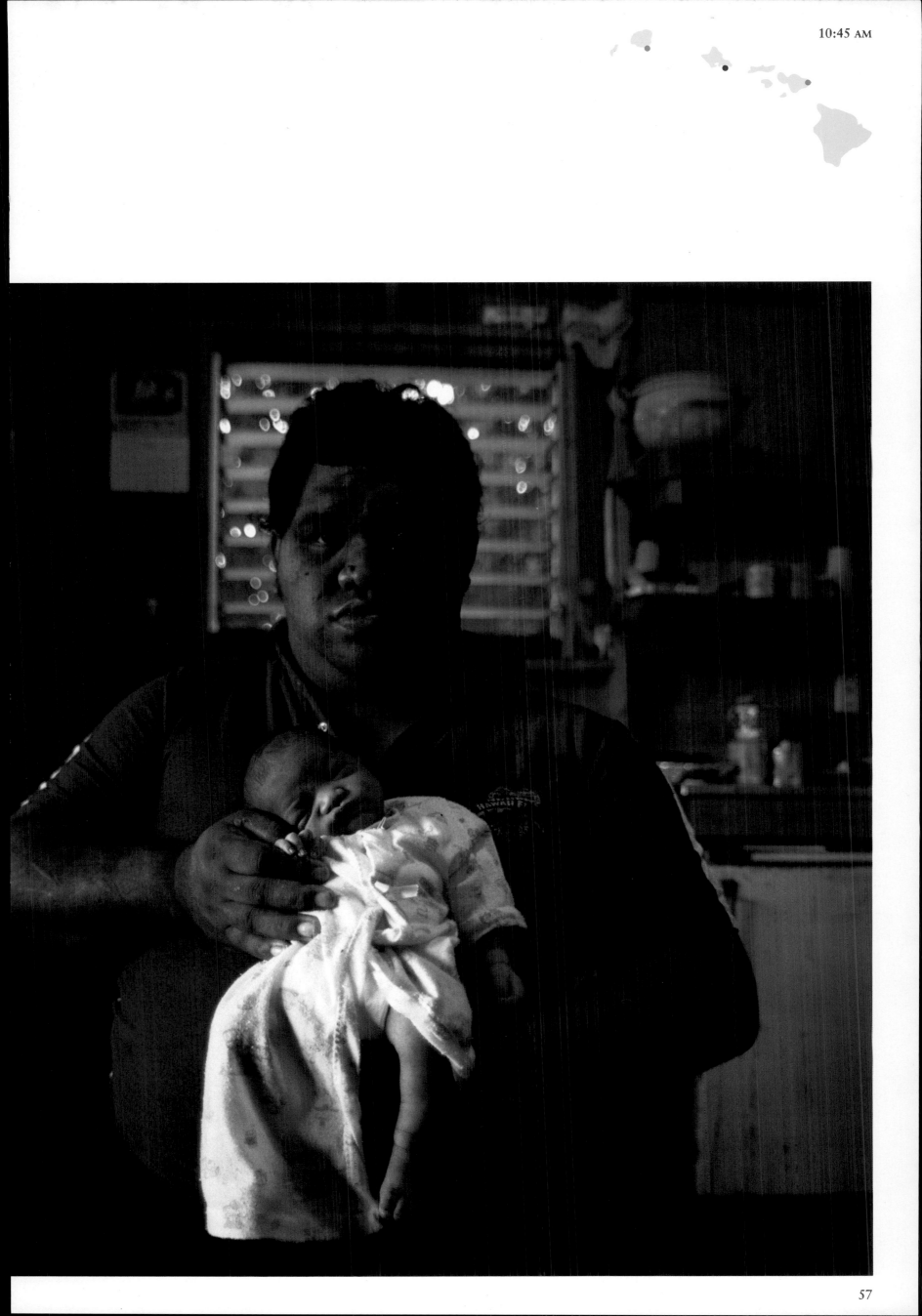

• *Left*

Vanessa Fukutani and six-month-old Holei wait for Dad to return to Hilo Bay from a fishing trip.

Photographer:
Jennifer Erwitt

• *Above*

Ben Aipa, 42, teaches his son Duke, 8, to surf on gentle waves at Haleiwa, Oahu. One of Hawaii's great surfers, Aipa named his son after the late Duke Kahanamoku, an Olympic gold medalist swimmer in 1912 and the father of modern surfing.

Photographer:
Aaron Chang

• *Above, top*

Phrendly (no last name) has been in Pahoa, Hawaii for three years. With him, his girlfriend Robin and her daughter Beany.

Photographer:
Matthew Naythons

Left

The Long Term Care Center, Wilcox Memorial Hospital, Kauai.

Photographer:
Sebastiao Salgado

Below

Careful steps toward a late-morning swim in the gentle 77° waters of Waikiki.

Photographer:
Matthew Naythons

Following page

At the Honolulu Zoo.

Photographer:
Donna Ferrato

Donna Ferrato

Richfield Livestock Auction
SALE EVERY WEDNESDAY

• *Below*

Visitors at the vast Polynesian Cultural Center in Laie don Tahitian tamure gear for a souvenir snapshot. The Mormon-run, nonprofit center is one of the most popular tour-bus stops in the state.

Photographer:
Alon Reininger

• *Below, right*

Over 700,000 Japanese tourists visited Hawaii in 1983. After a half-day bus tour of Oahu, the men in this tour group photograph the women at a beach park on Maunalua Bay.

Photographer:
Jean-Pierre Laffont

• *Right*

Sightseeing by water tricycle on Kailua Bay, the Big Island.

Photographer:
Diego Goldberg

Following page
quiet moment in down-
wn Hilo.
otographer:
i Reed

Eli Reed

• *Left*
Lunchtime touch-ups in the girls' restroom at Sacred Hearts Academy, Honolulu.
Photographer:
P. F. Bentley

• *Below*
The Big Island School of Ha
Design, Hilo.
Photographer:
William Albert Allard

• *Below*

An increasing number of couples from Japan combine weddings and honeymoons in Waikiki, where packaged ceremonies—including limousines, gowns and tuxedos, flowers, even churches—can be arranged for less than $500. One quarter of these assembly-line nuptials are "omiai" or arranged pairings. "It's like a blind date," says the limousine's driver Masao Minei. "If it's mutually agreeable, they have a wedding."

Photographer:
Jodi Cobb

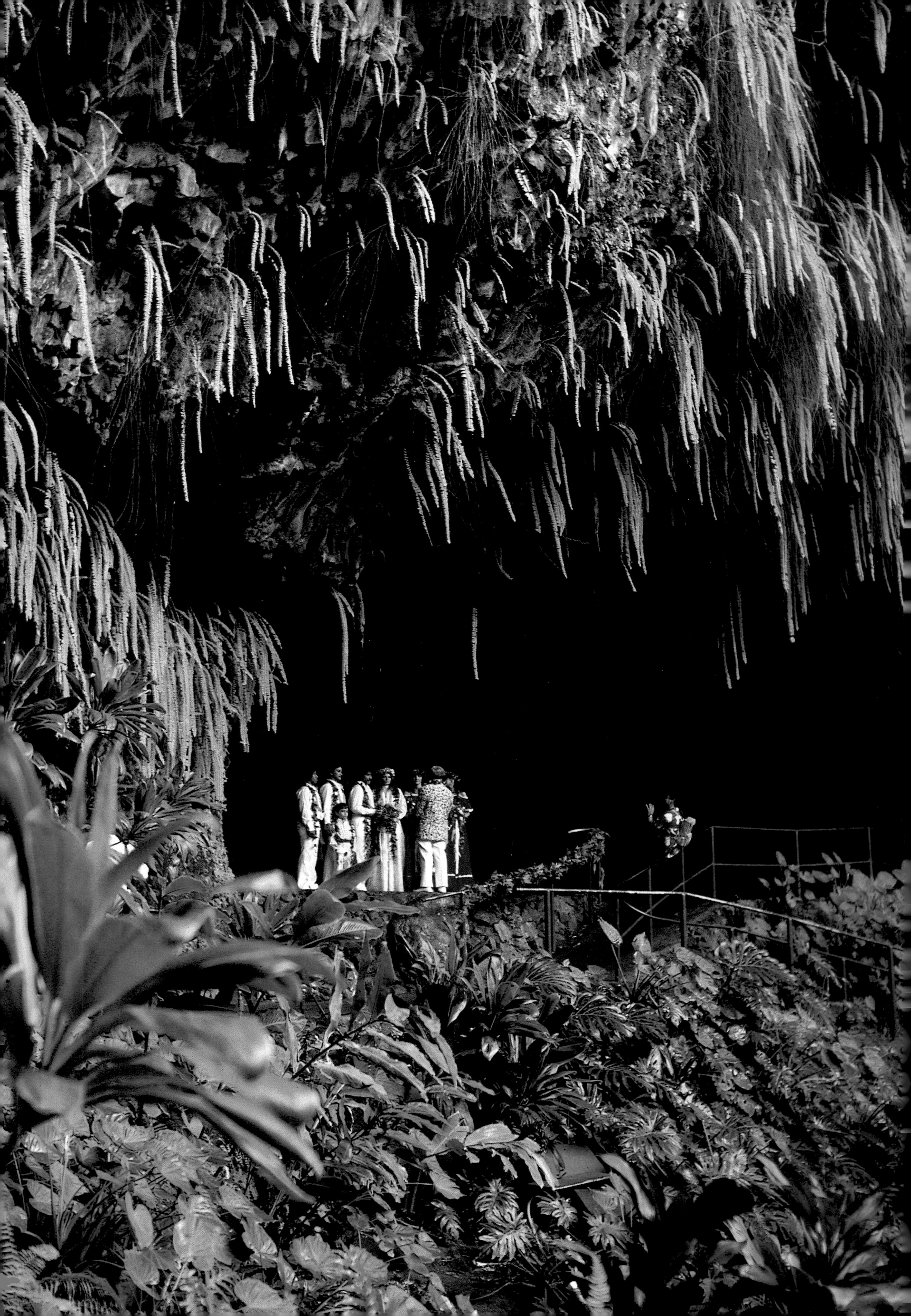

• *Left*

Joey Basconcillo, 29, a Filipino musician, and Canadian Mary Budd, 29, celebrate their marriage ceremony at the popular Fern Grotto on the island of Kauai.

Approximately 50 percent of all marriages in Hawaii are interracial. On December 2, thirty-two couples were married and the Honolulu courts finalized eleven divorce proceedings.

Photographer:
Dirck Halstead

• *Above*

Young love at Sandy Beach, a local sun and surf hangout on the suburban southeast end of Oahu.

Photographer:
David Alan Harvey

HALEIWA

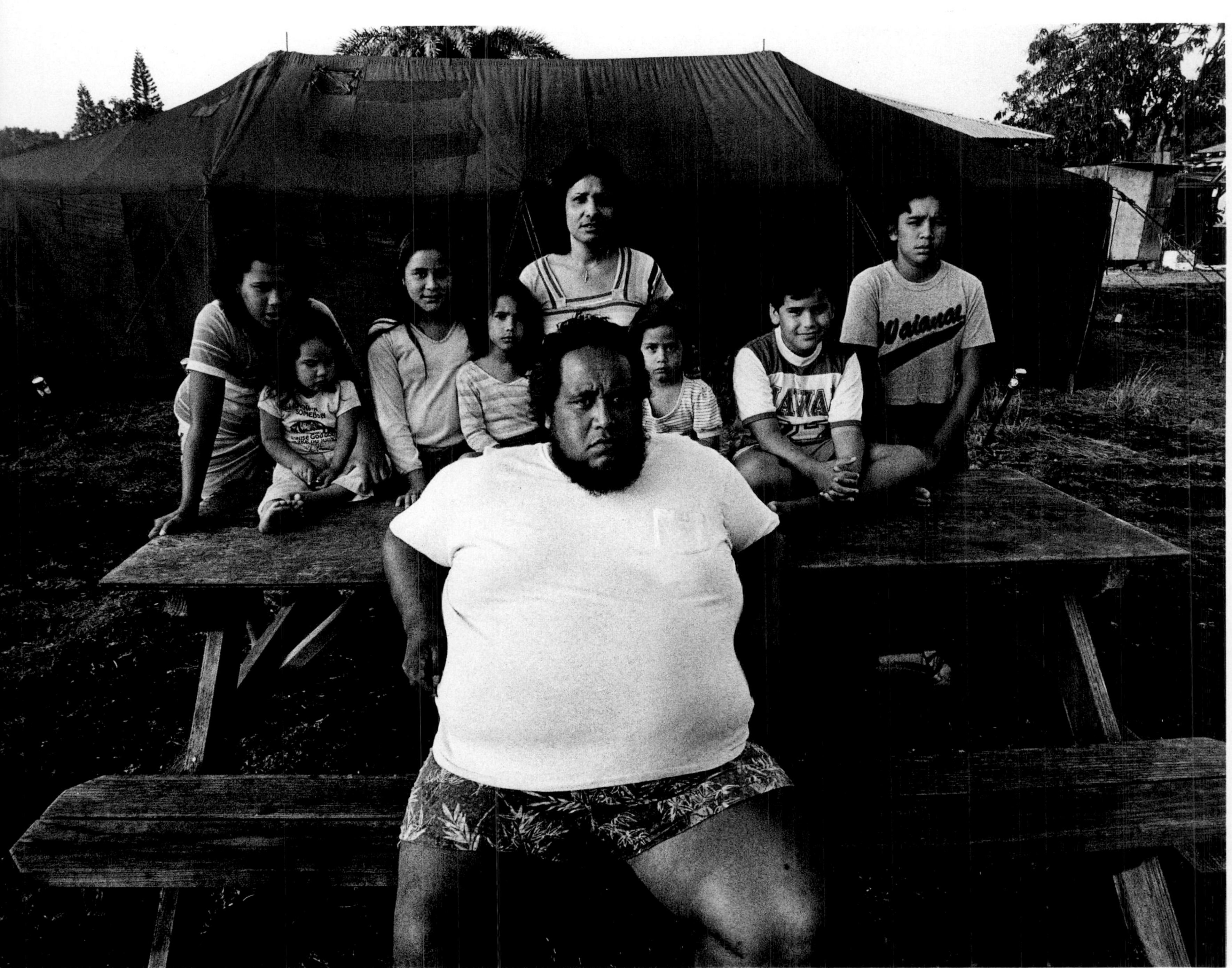

• *Left*

Sunshine Nichol and her husband Mark own Natural Arts of Hawaii, a surf shop in Haleiwa on Oahu's North Shore. Sunshine grew up in the Honolulu suburb of Ewa Beach. Mark is a New Yorker who moved to Hawaii in 1975 with a backpack and a hundred dollars to buy a surfboard.

Photographer:
Wayne Levin

• *Above*

Wendell Kahaleoumi, a teacher at Waianae High School, and his family live in a tent in Makaha on the Waianae coast of Oahu. Inside the big tent are two smaller tents for privacy. The Kahaleoumi home is one block from the beach and the weather is good all year round. Behind Wendell, left to right: Wendell Jr. ("Buffy"), Michele, Anna, Pualani, wife Anita, Mana, Kurtis and Ryan.

Photographer:
Arthur Grace

• *Following page*

Kenso Takamoto, 72, of Kukuihaele, Hawaii.

Photographer:
John Loengard

John Loengard

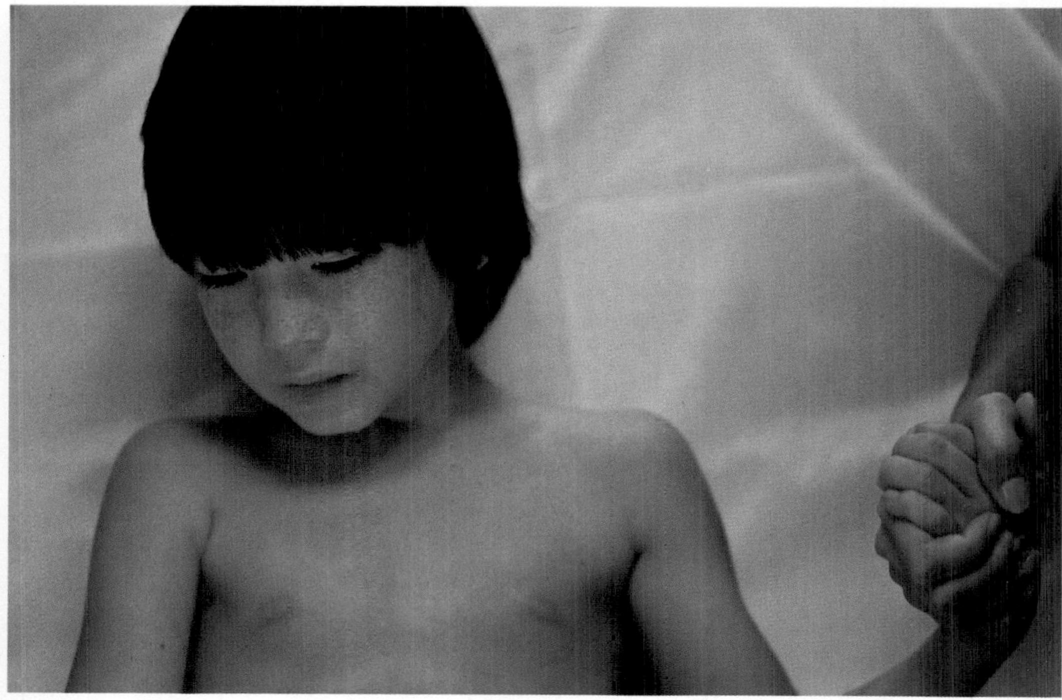

• *Left*

Dr. Alan Kaufman performs an operation on a quarter horse at Veterinary Associates, Inc. in Waimea, the ranching center of the Big Island.

Photographer:
Mark S. Wexler

• *Above*

In the emergency room of Queens Hospital, Honolulu, Ronne Castro of Kaimuki gets stitches for a cut on his right hand.

Photographer:
Jodi Cobb

• *Above*

A Hawaiian cowboy, or paniolo, cuts cattle on his "Japanese quarterhouse" at Kahua Ranch in Kohala, Hawaii.

Photographer:
Mark S. Wexler

• *Right*

Misha and Mindy Laney go for a ride with their grandfather, Ernest Richardson, on the island of Lanai.

Photographer:
Rich Clarkson

Since 1825, sugar cane has played a leading role in the economic and social life of Hawaii. Today, the sugar industry cultivates 200,000 acres on four islands, employs 9,000 people and produces Hawaii's leading export.

Hawaii's remarkable ethnic mix is the result of the sugar industry's century-long need for field workers. The first boatload of Chinese immigrant workers arrived in 1852. Japanese, Puerto Rican, Portuguese, Filipino and other groups followed. They worked the fields and eventually built new lives in Hawaii. The sugar plantation camps became Hawaii's Ellis Island.

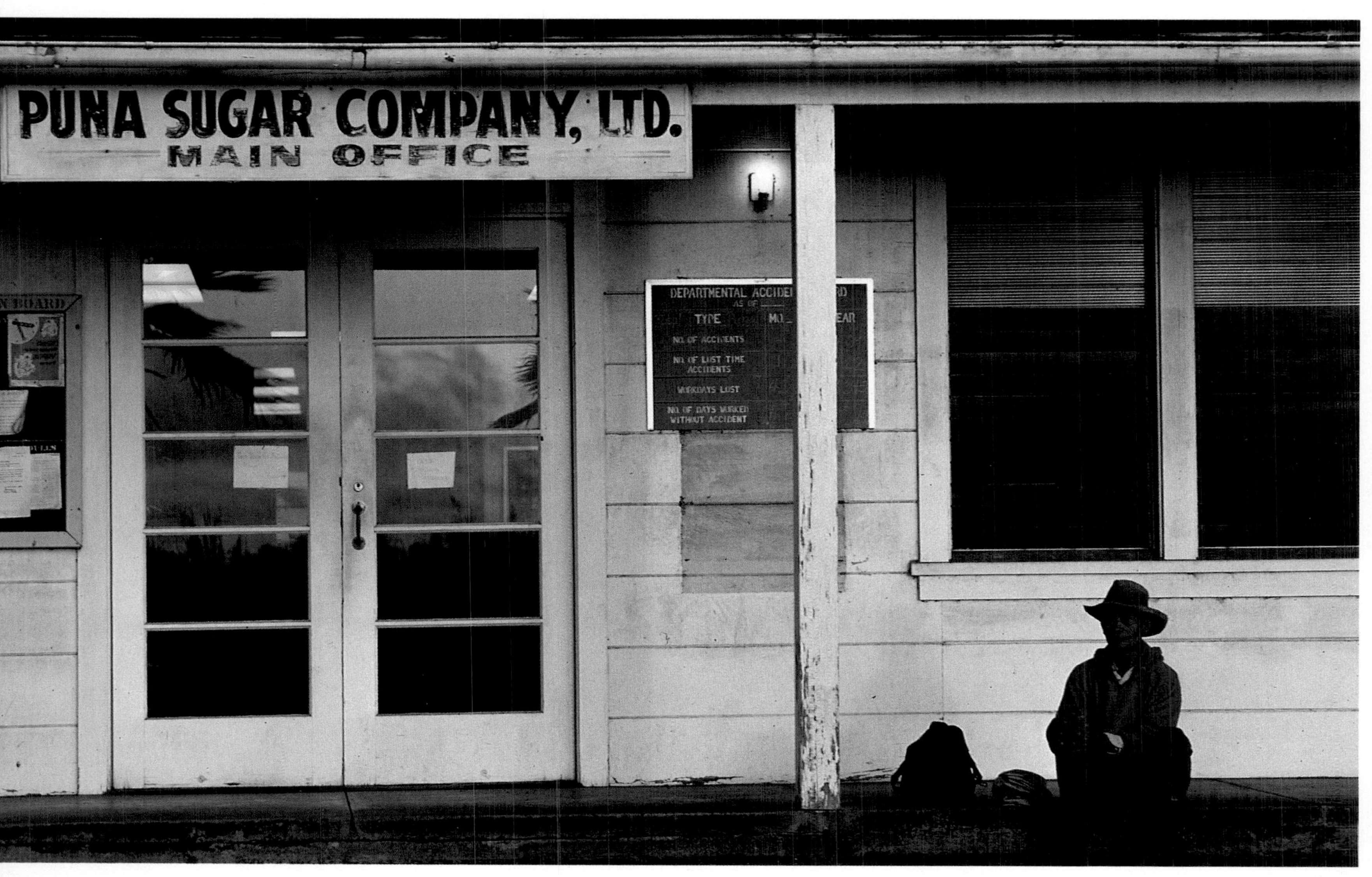

• *Left*

"The change from an economy where sugar was the main industry to a tourism-based economy is reflected in a brief moment when a United Airlines direct flight from San Francisco to Maui—a service initiated in December, 1982—flies over the 83-year-old Hawaiian Commercial & Sugar Company mill at Puunene."

Photography contest winner:
Gaylord C. Kubota

• *Above*

On one of Puna's last days, a sugar worker spends a moment sitting on the stoop of the old company office.

Photographer:
Matthew Naythons

The industry now faces an uncertain future. Labor costs, real-estate pressures, competition from foreign producers and reduced demand have all worked to squeeze the profit margins of Hawaii's sugar plantations.

Puna Sugar Company is one of fifteen major sugar plantations in Hawaii. Headquartered in the town of Keaau on the Big Island, Puna employs 29 people to cultivate, harvest and mill 12,000 acres of cane.

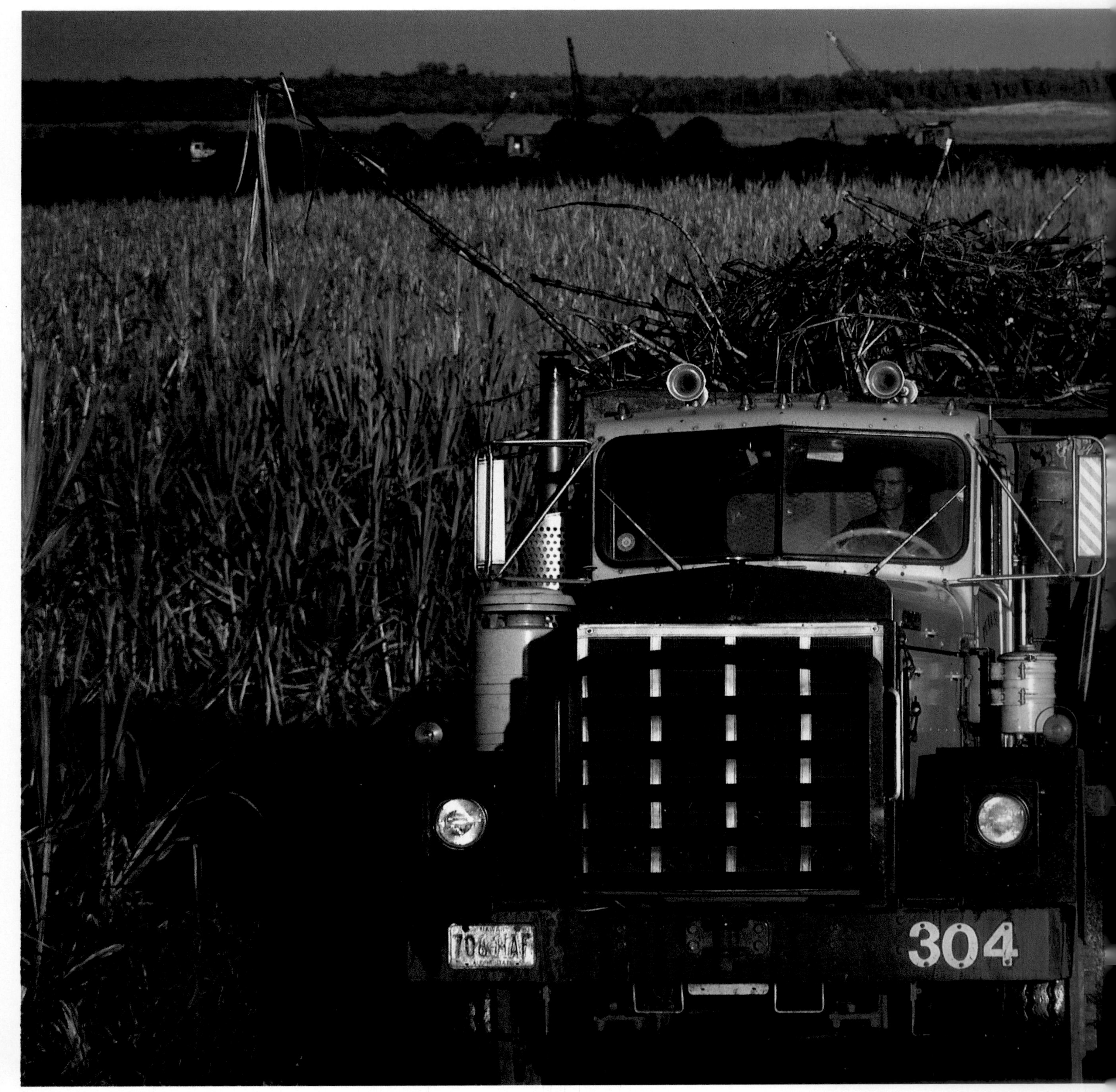

In January 1982, Puna Sugar's parent company, .mfac, Inc., announced the closing of the planta-on, effective as of September 1984, citing real and rojected losses. These photographs by Matthew Jaythons illustrate one of Puna's last harvests.

ıoto essay by Matthew Naythons

• *Left*

A truck hauls harvested cane from the fields near Mountain View to the Puna Sugar Mill in Keaau. At the mill, the raw cane is chopped, pressed, clarified, boiled and spun into brown raw sugar. The raw sugar travels to California where it is refined and packaged into household sugar, powdered sugar for bakers, brown sugar and liquid sugar used by canners and soft-drink manufacturers.

• *Above, top*

A cane truck driver waits while harvesters load one of the last cane crops these fields will bear. Less-than-perfect soil conditions and an overabundance of rain were crucial factors in the decision to close the Puna plantation.

• *Above*

Mature cane is burned to strip off leaves prior to harvesting.

• *Above*

The sun shines on Oahu beaches 22 days in the month of December, a statistic that does not seem to please everyone.

Photographer:
David Alan Harvey

• *Right*

The Whaler Cove show at Sea Life Park, Oahu.

Photographer:
Jean-Pierre Laffont

• *Following page*

"Hawai'i Ka U Kumu" ("Hawaii Is My Teacher"), a mural completed by local artist Calley O'Neill in 1982, animates a corner of the Campus Center at the University of Hawaii, Honolulu.

Photographer:
P. F. Bentley

P.E. Bentley

• *Left*
Sunset Beach, Oahu.
Photographer:
Aaron Chang

• *Above*
Snack time at Kamaka Pond, a bathing pool used in lieu of plumbing by the residents of Milolii, Hawaii.
Photographer:
Diego Goldberg

• *Following pages*
Michael Evans, personal photographer to President Ronald Reagan, set up a makeshift studio in the Sheraton Waikiki Hotel. On December 2, he invited Honolulu residents to have their portraits taken:
Page 92
Office Coordinator Reva Uso and her son, Tafiti.
Page 93
Halekulani Hotel training manager Randie O'Shaughnessy and her son, Seamus.
Page 94
Christopher, Walter and Peter Dods.
Page 95
Silent film star and legendary resident of The Royal Hawaiian Hotel, Dorothy Mackaill.
Photographer:
Michael Evans

Michael Evans

Michael Evans

Michael Evans

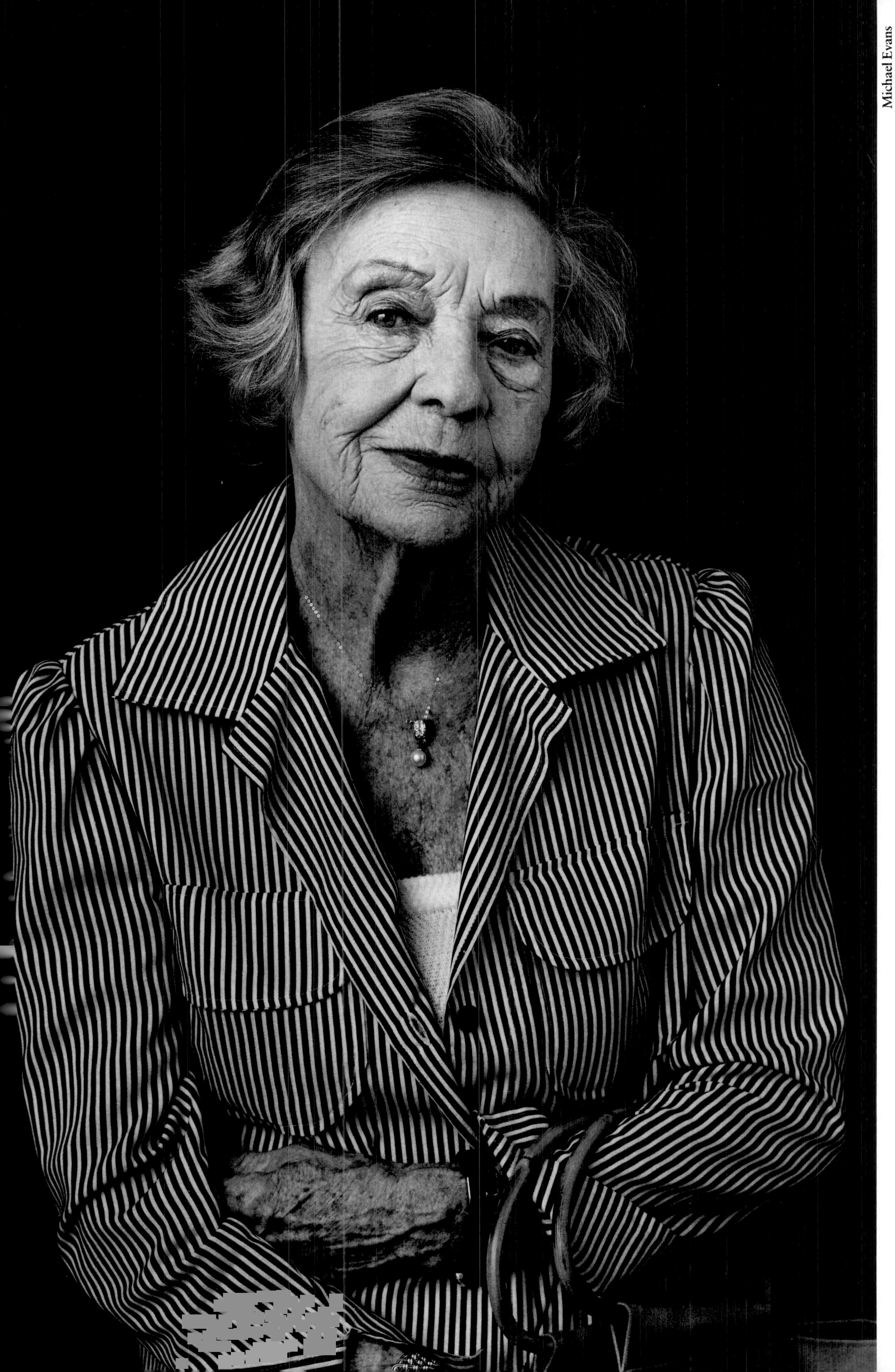

Michael Evans

Rene Burri

1:30 PM

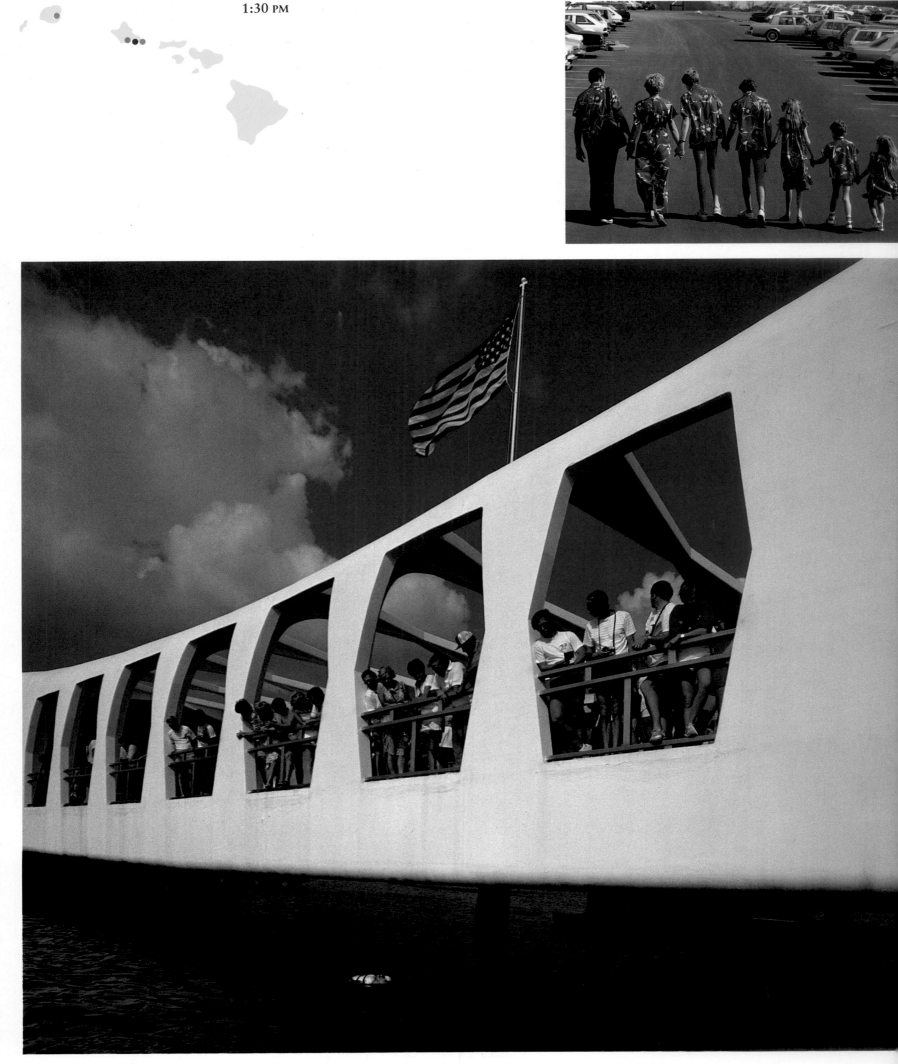

• *Previous page*

During their visit from Calgary, Canada, Lilian Mah and Helen Wei take time to shop at Honolulu's huge Ala Moana Shopping Center.

Photographer:
Rene Burri

• *Above, top*

The Schauerhamer family, visiting from Utah.

Photographer:
Jean-Pierre Laffont

• *Above*

Those who remember (and those who don't) peer down at the sunken hulk of the USS Arizona, visible a few feet beneath the placid surface of Pearl Harbor. A white marble memorial straddles the behemoth, one of eight American battleships crippled or destroyed by Japanese bombers at Pearl Harbor on December 7, 1941. Eleven hundred Navy men went down with the Arizona, which still sends up small, rainbow-colored oil slicks.

Photographer:
Dennis Oda

• *Right*

The "Garden Island" of Kauai is a cinematographer paradise (*South Pacific, The Thorn Birds, Raiders of the Lost Ark*). Breath-taking Wailua Falls has been wide seen in the opening credits the popular U.S. television series, "Fantasy Island."

Photographer:
Wilbur E. Garrett

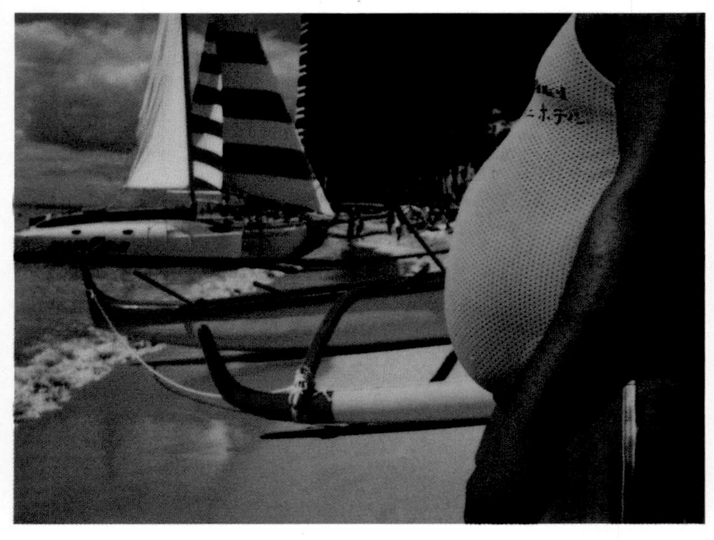

Matthew Naythons

Matthew Naythons

Gregory Heisler

Diego Goldberg

David Cohen

Rick Smolan

Arnaud deWildenberg

Matthew Naythons

• *Above*

Waikiki Beach, 1:27 PM.
Waikiki Beach, 1:30 PM.
Photographer:
Rick Smolan

• *Right*

Waikiki, perhaps the most famous beach resort in the world, is also a miracle mile of hotels, shops, restaurants and clubs that attract visitors from all over the world.
Photographer:
Gerd Ludwig

WATERMAN

• *Left*

Holding the pose for a self-timed camera in Waikiki.

Photographer:
Alon Reininger

• *Above*

Yorihito Uchida photographs his patrons and mounts their pictures on the walls of his eating and drinking establishment on Maui. Practically every inch of wall space in Yori's Tavern has been filled.

Photographer:
Rick Smolan

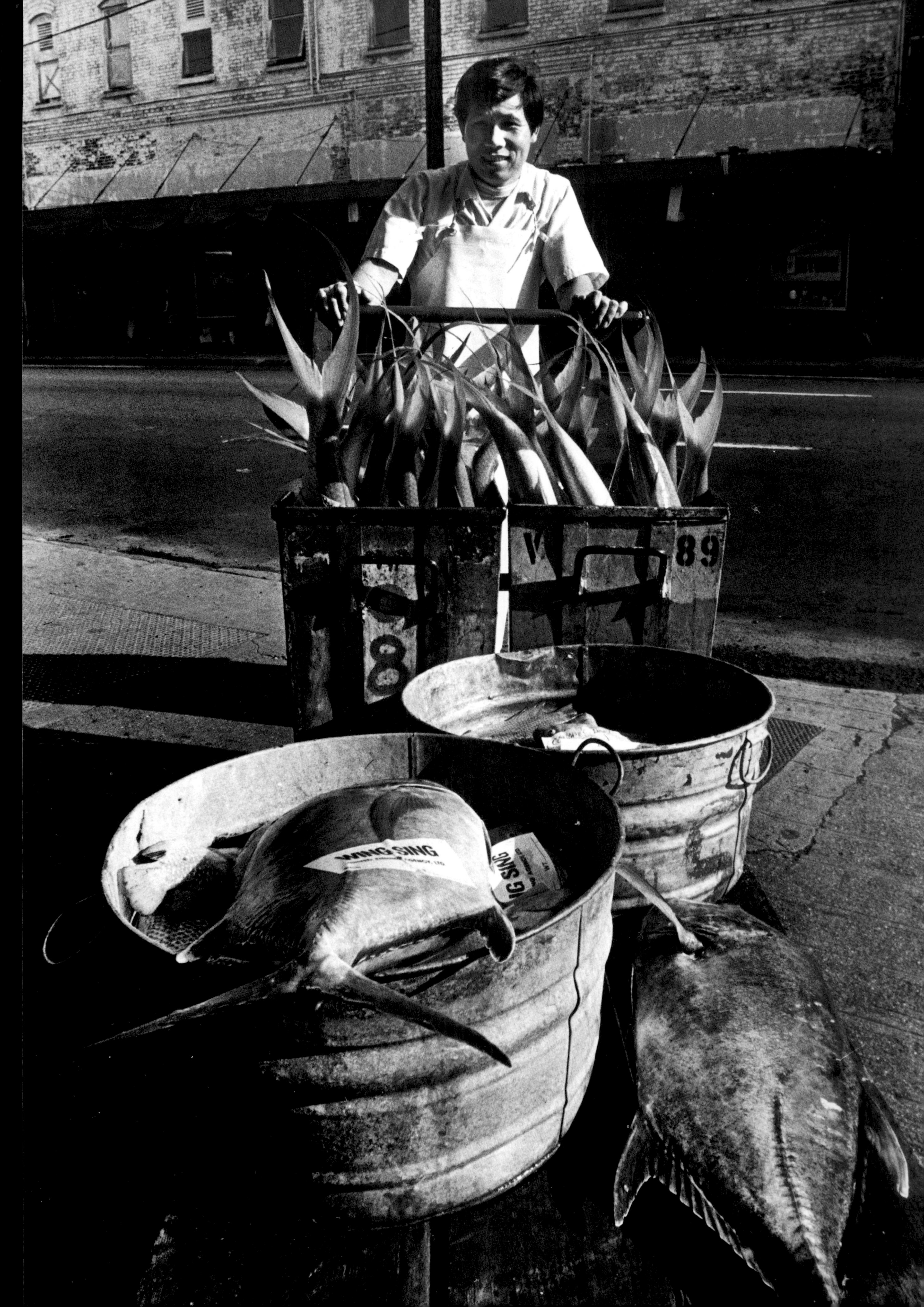

89
WING SING

The *Honolulu Advertiser* and the Eastman Kodak Company issued a challenge to amateur photographers throughout Hawaii: "Dust off your cameras on December 2 and match your photographic skills against fifty of the world's top photojournalists." A host of talented amateurs accepted the challenge and entered their best efforts in the "Day in the Life" photography contest. In some cases, the amateur photographs were as good as or better than those taken by the professionals.

One of the winners, John Young, had a slight advantage. He was the mission commander of the NASA space shuttle Columbia. His winning photographs, shot as the shuttle passed over Hawaii, appear on page 132–133. Here are some other winning photographs.

Ship at Sunrise.
Photographer: Milton Diamond

Playing on the back lanai.
Photographer: Edith Suganama

Sunrise at Bigelow's Pier, Kaneohe Bay, Oahu.
Photographer: Karen Suenaga

Leleiwi Trail, Haleakala Crater, Maui.
Photographer: Arthur Farinas

A private moment at Hanauma Bay, Oahu.
Photographer: Masami Teraoka

Hula lessons.
Photographer: Michael T. Saruwatari

Left
At the fish market, Honolulu, Oahu.
Photographer: Christopher C. Ray

• *Left*

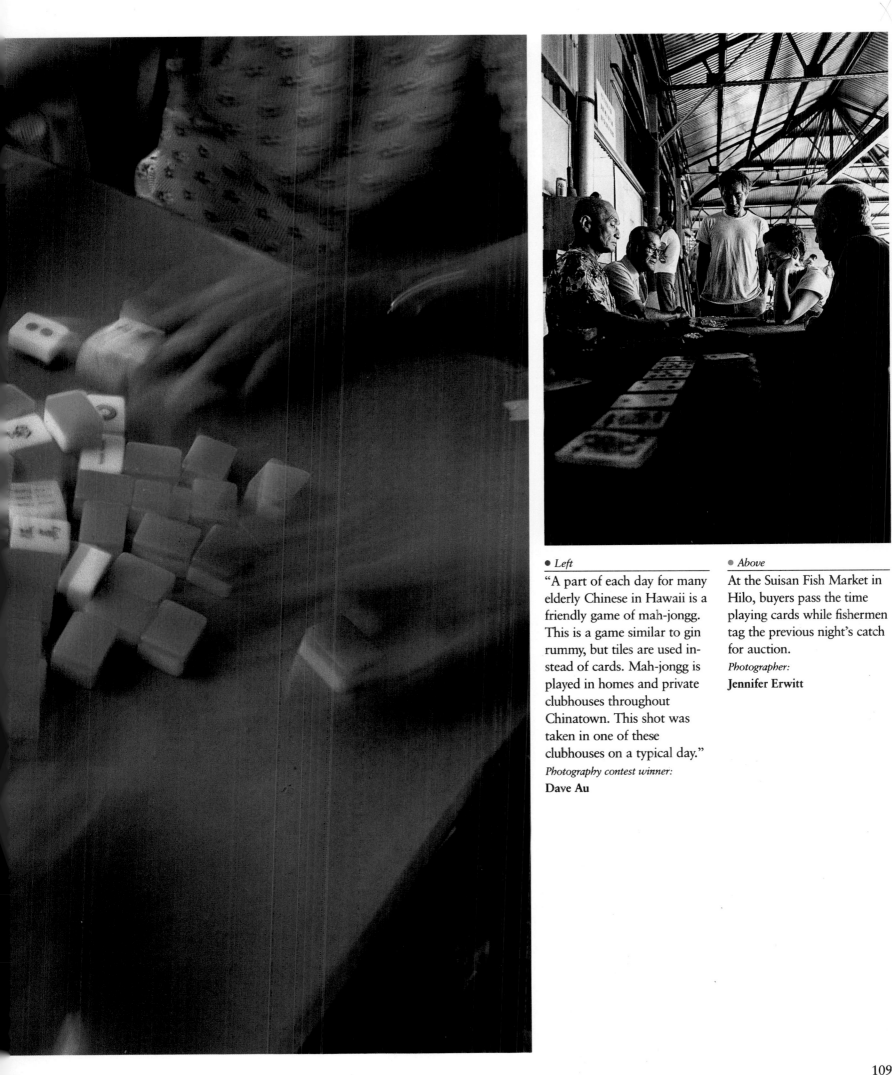

"A part of each day for many elderly Chinese in Hawaii is a friendly game of mah-jongg. This is a game similar to gin rummy, but tiles are used instead of cards. Mah-jongg is played in homes and private clubhouses throughout Chinatown. This shot was taken in one of these clubhouses on a typical day."

Photography contest winner:
Dave Au

• *Above*

At the Suisan Fish Market in Hilo, buyers pass the time playing cards while fishermen tag the previous night's catch for auction.

Photographer:
Jennifer Erwitt

• *Left*

Retired sugar-plantation manager Harlow Wright and his wife Marion, 40-year residents of Lahaina, Maui.

Photographer:

Stephanie Maze

• *Above*

Waikiki.

Photographer:

William Albert Allard

• *Following page*

Kuhio Park Terrace, a high-rise public housing project built in Honolulu in the 1960s, houses one of the largest concentrations of Samoans outside Samoa.

Photographer:

Abbas

Abbas

Michael O'Brien

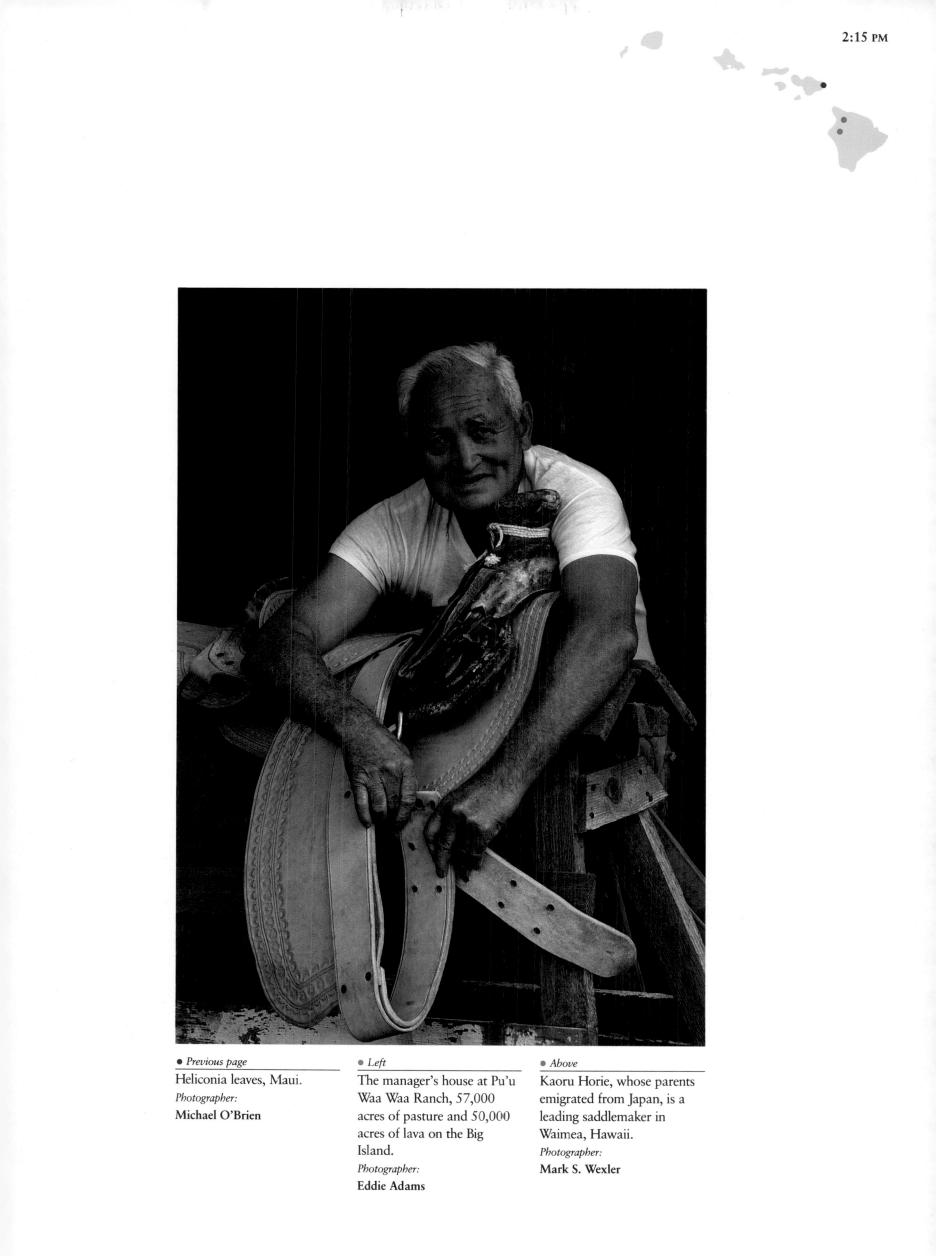

• *Previous page*
Heliconia leaves, Maui.
Photographer:
Michael O'Brien

• *Left*
The manager's house at Pu'u Waa Waa Ranch, 57,000 acres of pasture and 50,000 acres of lava on the Big Island.
Photographer:
Eddie Adams

• *Above*
Kaoru Horie, whose parents emigrated from Japan, is a leading saddlemaker in Waimea, Hawaii.
Photographer:
Mark S. Wexler

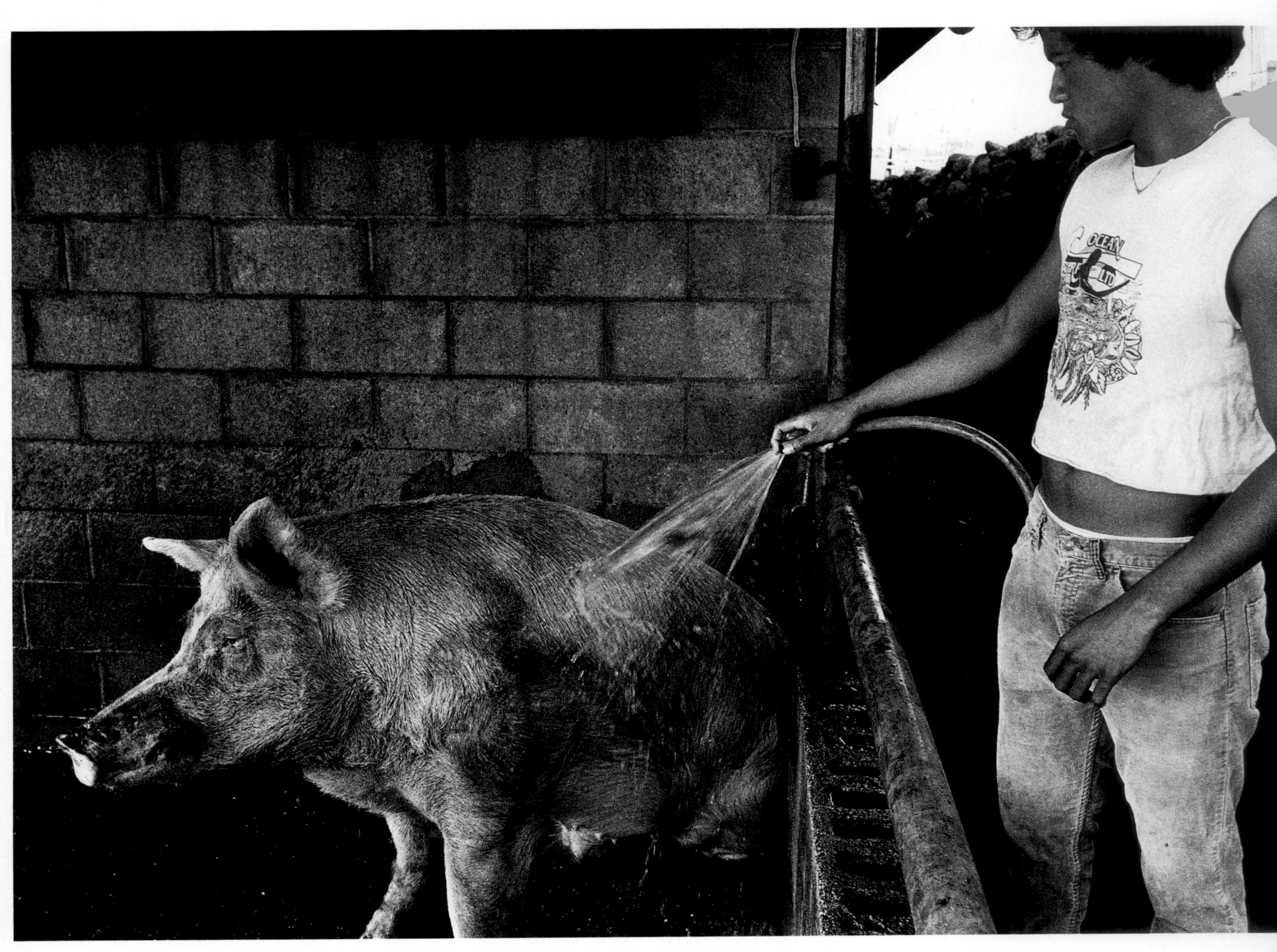

• *Above*

Raising livestock is part of the unusual curriculum for boarding students at Lahainaluna High School, Maui.

Photographer:
Bob Davis

• *Right*

A herd dog takes a break after a long day rounding up cattle at Kahuku Ranch on the Big Island.

Photographer:
Sam Garcia

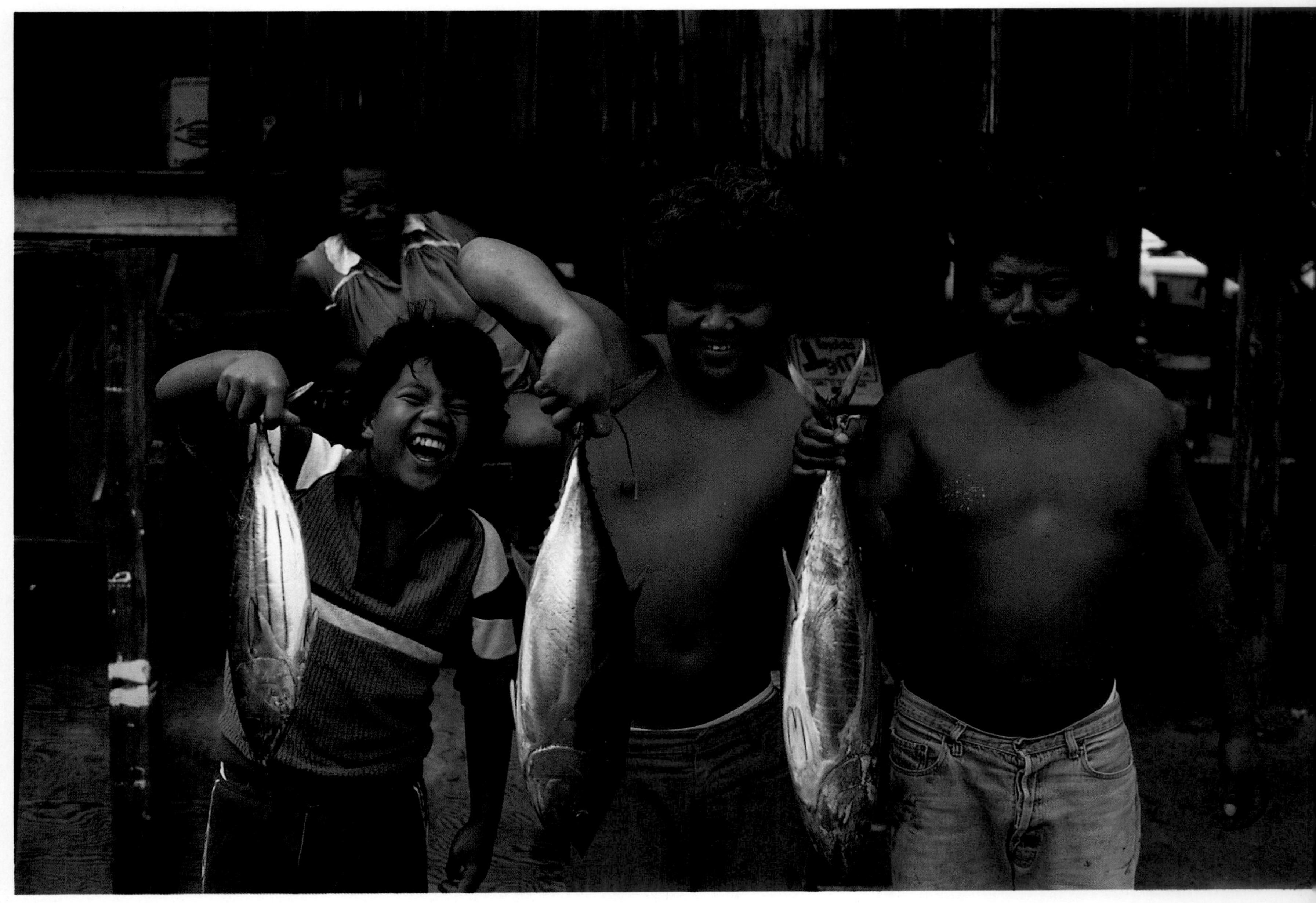

• *Above*

The Martinez family of Milolii displays part of the day's tuna catch, which they will sell directly to a local supermarket.

Photographer:

Diego Goldberg

• *Right*

A spotted moray eel, roused from his hole in the reef off Molokini Island, gapes at marine photographer David Doubilet. Nocturnal feeders, moray eels poke into crevices and cracks for sleeping prey. Their only enemies are large jacks and sharks. The spotted or dragon moray is thought to be the most intelligent of Hawaiian fishes.

Photographer:

David Doubilet

• *Left*

The motto of the Kaneohe Maintenance and Operations Squadron fire-fighting team.

Photographer:
Allan Seiden

• *Following page*

Kalalau Beach on the fabled Na Pali coast of Kauai.

Photographer:
Wilbur E. Garrett

• *Above*

Aviation fuel floating on a pool of water is set afire, then extinguished, during a crash-and-rescue demonstration at Kaneohe Marine Corps Air Station.

Photographer:
Allan Seiden

• *Right*

At Honolulu International Airport, fire-turret practice drenches an old DC-6.

Photographer:
Robert Goodman

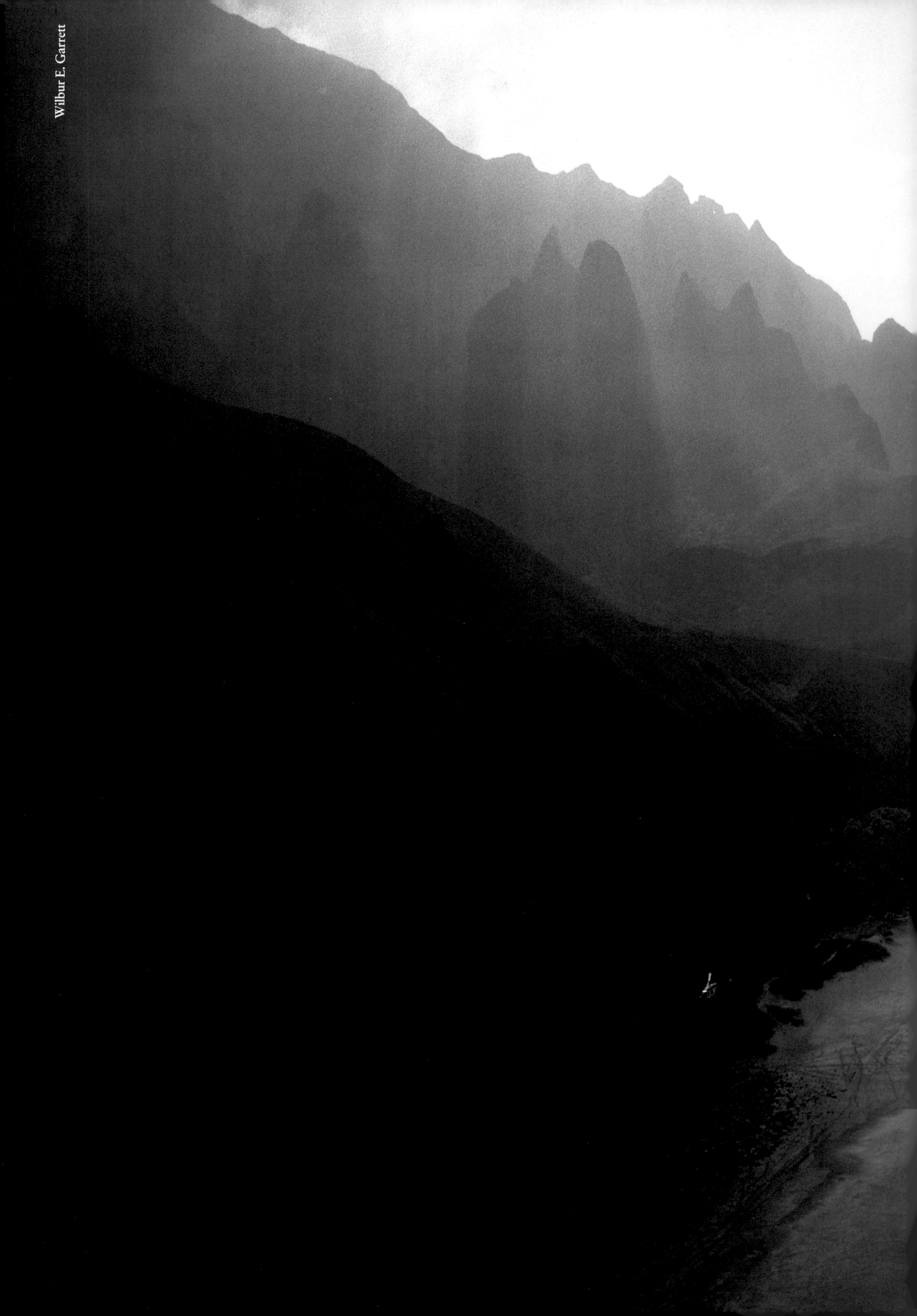

Wilbur E. Garrett

• *Above*

David Santopoalo, a grinder at weldshop 26-A, Pearl Harbor Naval Base.

Photographer:
Arnaud DeWildenberg

• *Right*

Dr. William Palmer makes a house call on John Hale (pronounced hah'-lay), a pure Hawaiian fisherman who lives at Pohoiki Bay in the Puna district of the Big Island.

Photographer:
Matthew Naythons

Above

Taxi stand and mural, Hilo.

3:30 PM

• *Above*

Kahua Ranch in the Kohala uplands of the Big Island.

Photographer:

Mark S. Wexler

John Loengard

• *Previous page*

Calbert Imada's father hunts wild pigs on the Big Island. Part of his collection of jaw bones is nailed to the wall behind Calbert.

Photographer:
John Loengard

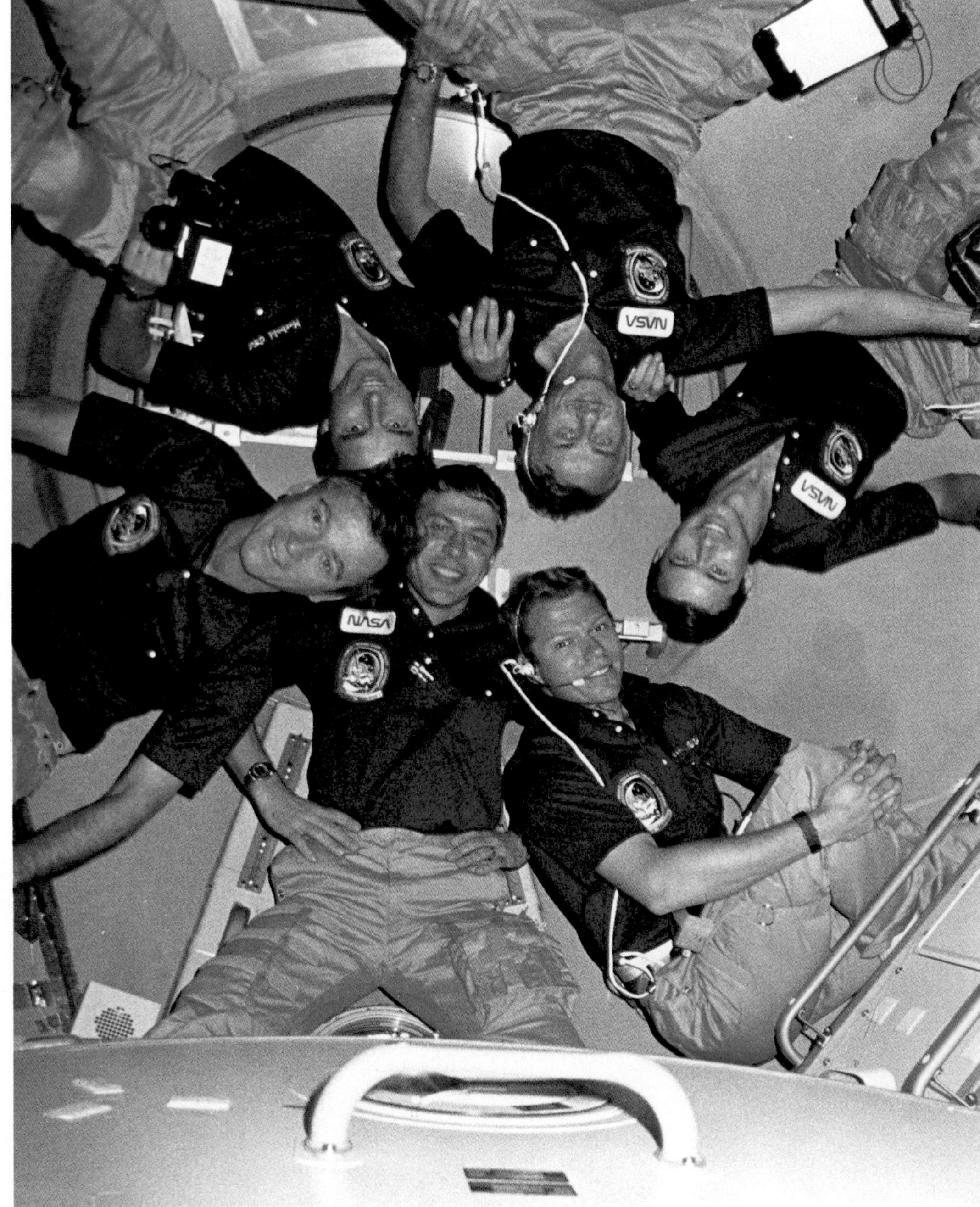

• *Above*

December 2 was the fourth day of the shuttle's ten-day mission. One hundred and fifty miles above the tracking station, the space shuttle crew poses for a low-gravity group portrait.

Photography contest winner:
John Young

• *Right*

Mission Commander John Young took several shots of Hawaii through Columbia's high-quality optical window with a 24-centimeter European Metric Camera, usually used for map making. The Big Island of Hawaii is at the top of the picture, the tip of Maui at the bottom.

Photography contest winner:
John Young

• *Right*

National Geographic Editor Bill Garrett happened to walk into the NASA tracking station at Kokee, Kauai just as the orbiting space shuttle Columbia passed over Hawaii. On the screens in the earth station control room are live direct transmissions from the spacecraft.

Photographer:
Wilber E. Garrett

David Doubilet

Dana Fineman

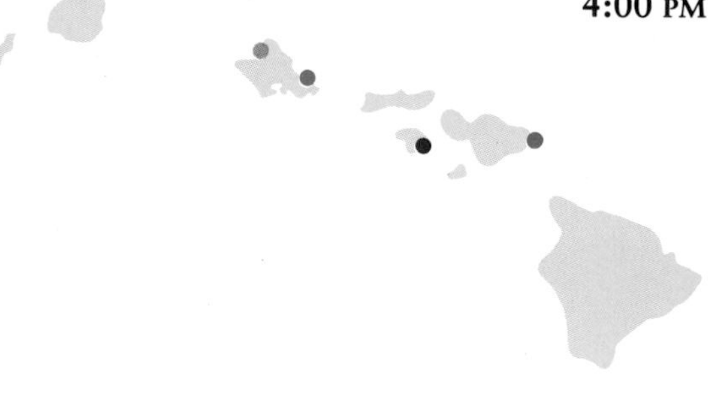

• *Previous pages 134–135*

Professional divers Eric Lefevre and Beth Gleason hang in the windows of the Second Cathedral, a cave off the island of Lanai.

Photographer:
David Doubilet

• *Previous pages 136–137*

Wally Amos strolls Lanikai Beach on Oahu with his wife and 12-week-old baby girl. "Famous Amos" cookies, launched in Hawaii, have become popular throughout the world, and Amos' smiling visage has become "the face that launched a thousand chips."

Photographer:
Dana Fineman

• *Above*

Tiny Malaikini, tour operator and entrepreneur, Hana, Maui.

Photographer:
Michael O'Brien

• *Right*

John Orlando applies fiberglass to the shaped foam cores of surfboards. Orlando is considered to be the top "glasser" on the North Shore.

Photographer:
Aaron Chang

TRIAD

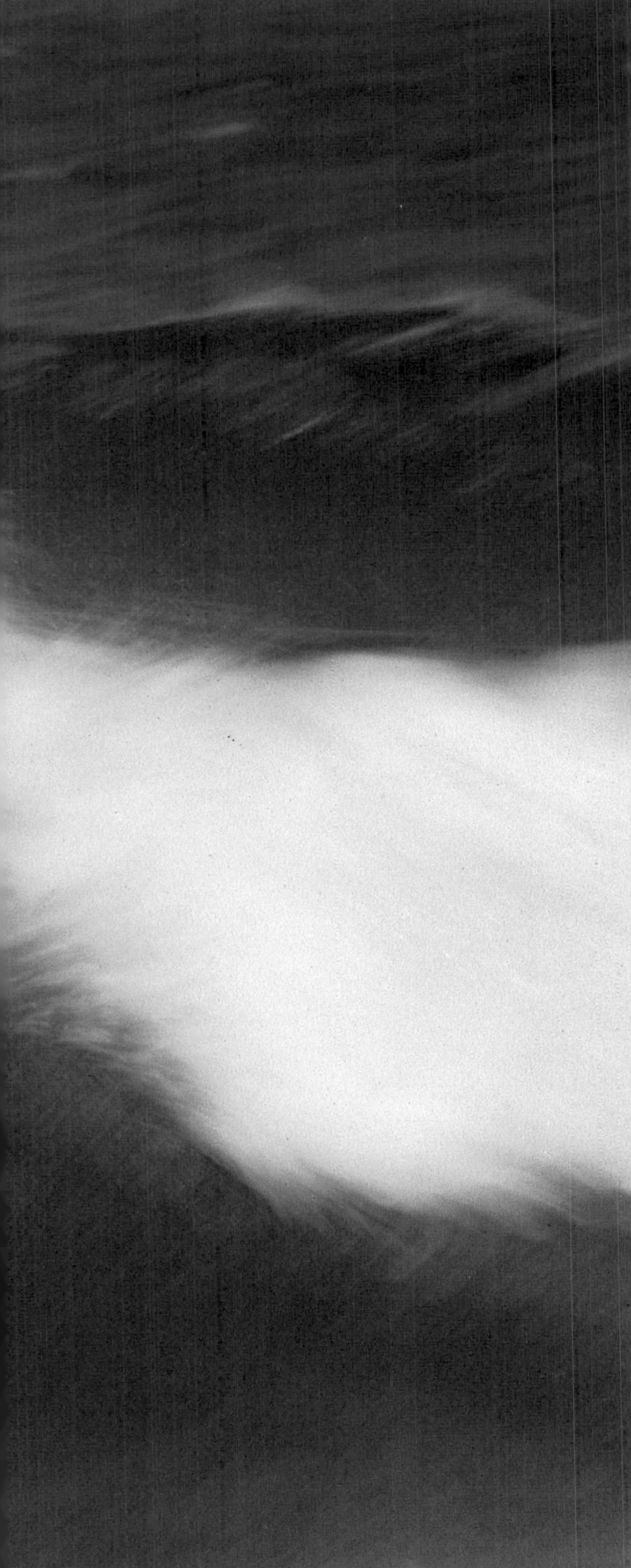

• *Far left*

Gusty conditions at Hookipa Bay on Maui, where the world's best big-surf wind surfer, Mike Waltze, slices a tough choreography across the face of a wave.

Photographer:
Steve Wilkings

• *Left*

Scott Manley, "wave-jumping" at Sandy Beach, Oahu. He says "it takes a lot of momentum" to get where he is in these pictures.

Photographer:
David Alan Harvey

• *Below, left*

On the playing fields at Punahou School, one of Honolulu's prestigious private day schools.

Photographer:

Carl Ganter

• *Below, right*

Twelve-year-old Eli Clemons goes "boogie-boarding" almost every day with his dad and brother. He likes "the rush of getting covered up inside the wave."

Photographer:

David Alan Harvey

• *Bottom, right*

Varsity girls swim practice at Punahou School.

Photographer:

Carl Ganter

• *Following page*

Fresh off Aloha Airlines flight 203 from Maui, the Pukalani Broncos gang up for a portrait at Honolulu International Airport. The Broncos were in town for a Pee Wee League football game against the Honolulu Punchbowls. On Saturday morning they played to a 6-6 tie.

Photographer:

Robert Goodman

Robert Goodman

HARLEY-DAVIDSO
22
35

• *Right*

A young hula dancer shows classic form on Molokai.

Photographer:

Dan Dry

• *Right*

"Every Friday afternoon after school, Maile Matsuura, 8, and Kerri Higa, 7, go to Yoshiko Nakasone's school for Okinawan dancing in Honolulu's Liliha neighborhood. Mrs. Nakasone has been teaching for 26 years and is one of just a handful of Okinawan dance teachers in Hawaii.

"In recent years, the local Okinawan community has experienced a surge of pride in its ethnic heritage, and a renewed interest in the dances of Okinawa has been one of the results."

Photography contest winner:

Michael Young

• *Right*

Students of the Connie Romani Dance School in Honolulu's affluent Kahala section wait for their ride after class.

Photographer:

Rick Smolan

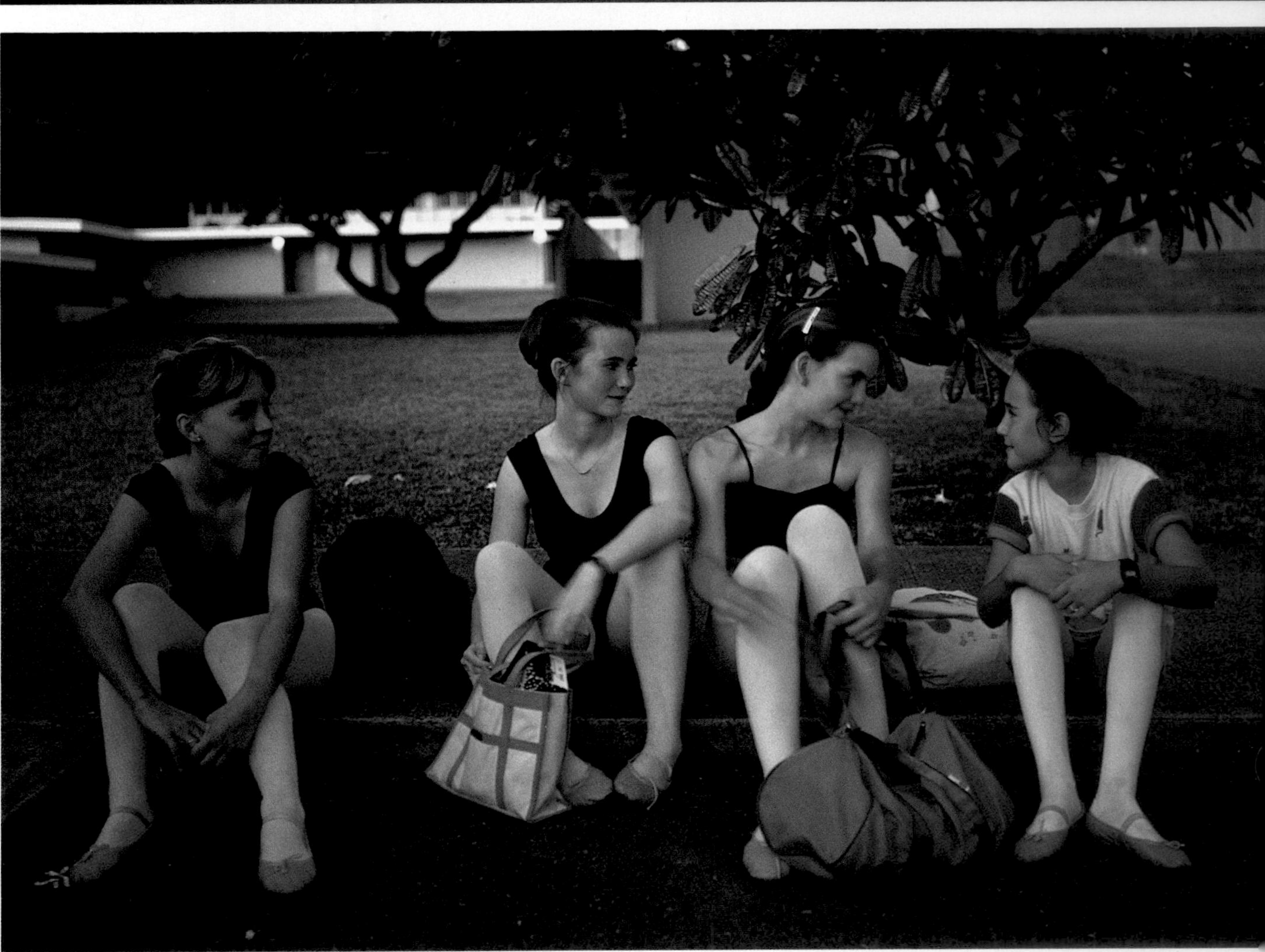

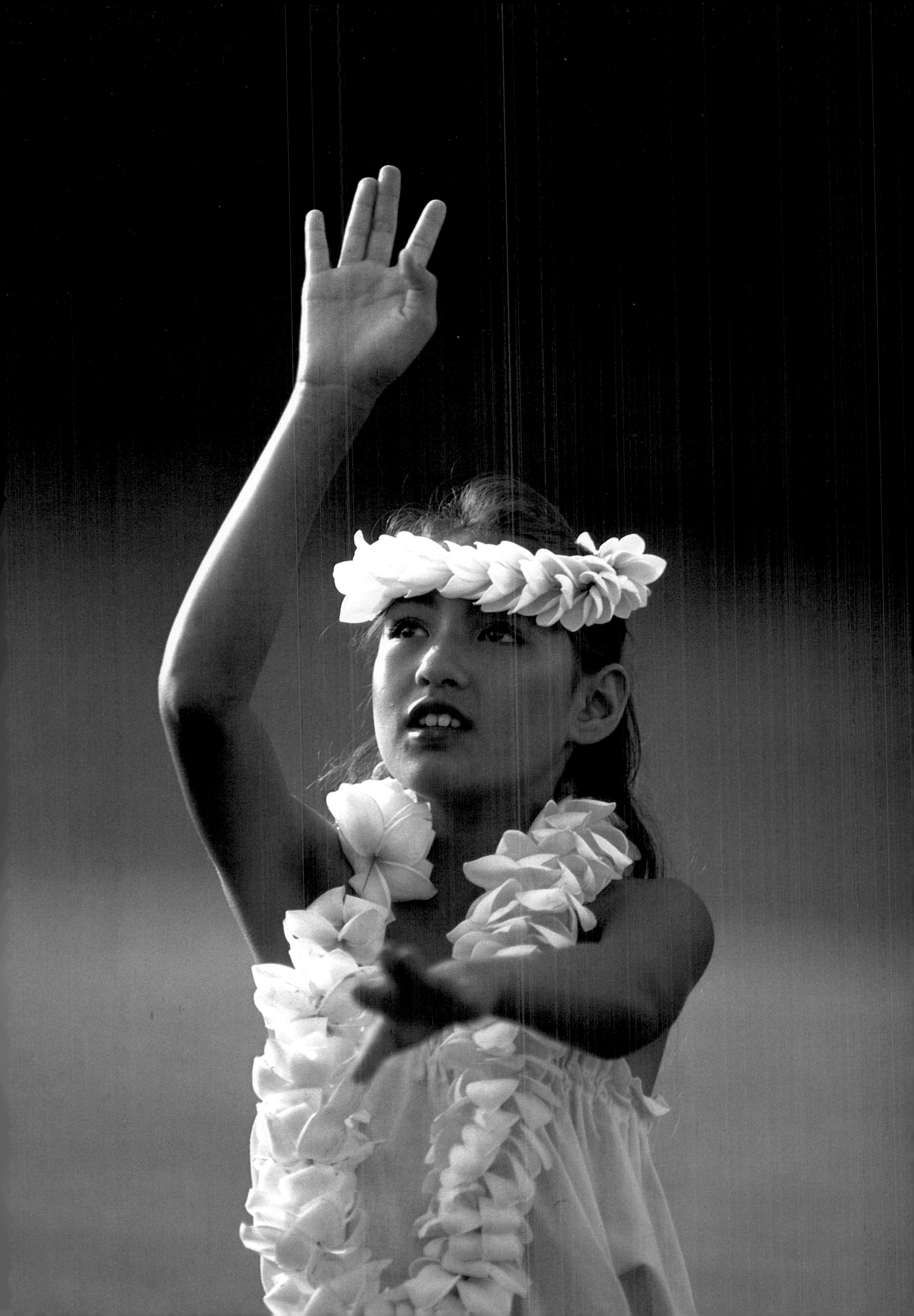

4:45 PM

• *Above*

Brothers and sisters on Waikiki Beach.

Photographer:

Donna Ferrato

supplied one hundred schoolchildren with disc cameras. In return for working on *A Day in the Life of Hawaii*, the children were allowed to keep their cameras. On this page is a selection from the 2,400 photographs shot by this army of young photographers.

Photographer: Tia Bryan, age 10

Photographer: Michelle Schauerhamer, age 11

Photographer: Jason Apilado, age 12

Photographer: Steven Kuahuia, age 14

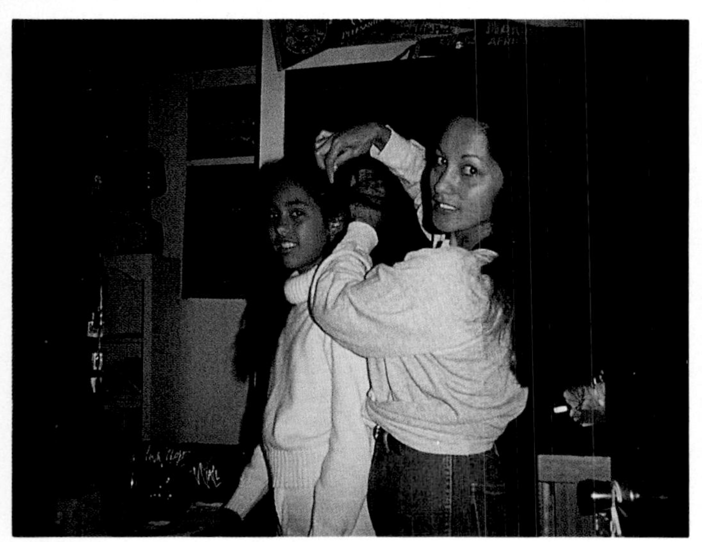

Photographer: William P. Tavaris, age 9

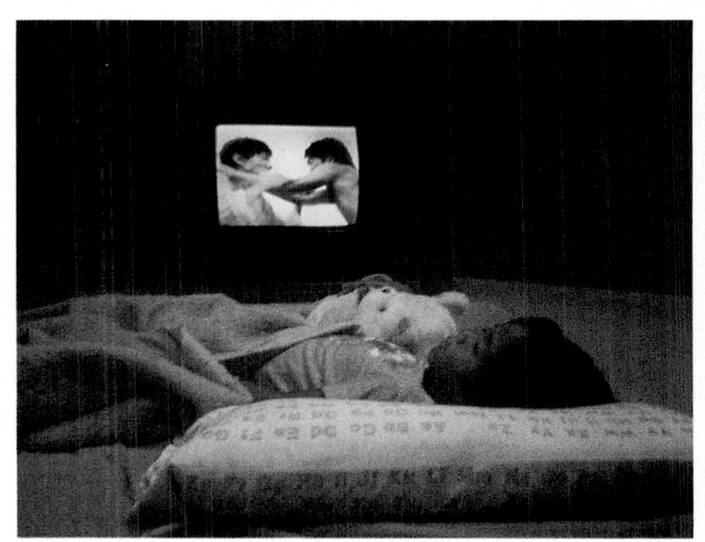

Photographer: Debbie Tomas, age 12

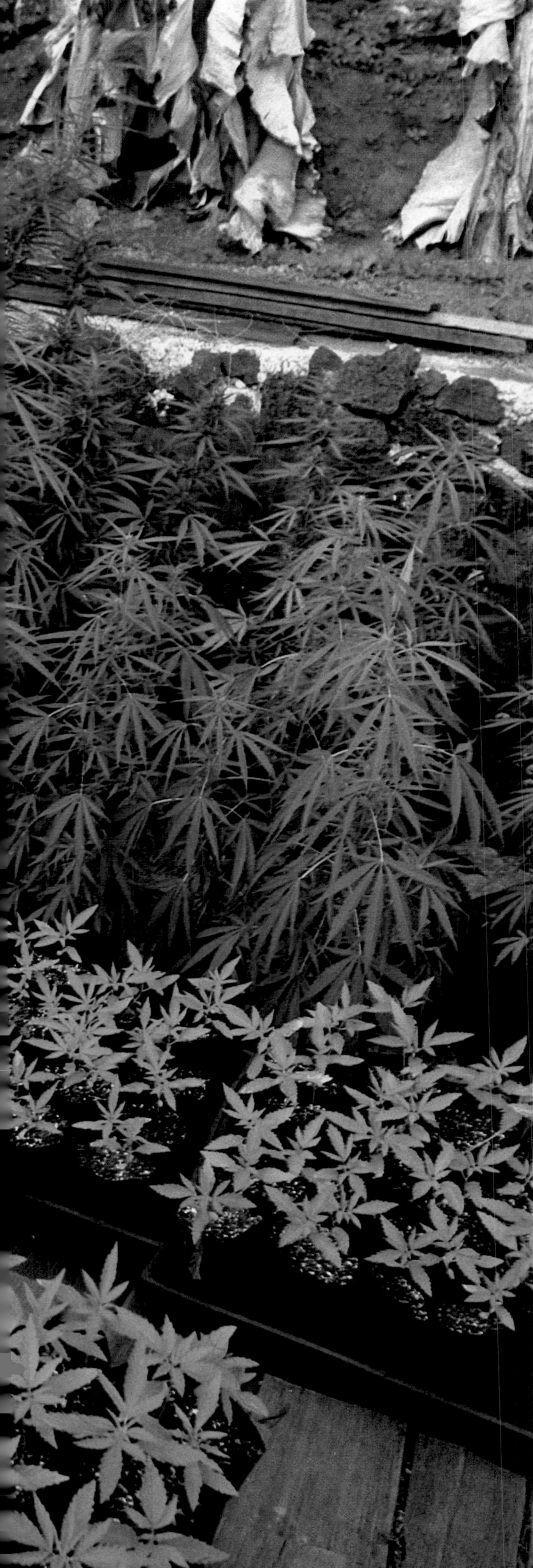

• *Left*

"Marijuana is a genuine cottage industry on the island of Kauai. In addition to a number of commercial growers, there are many more who have only a few plants. It's said here that there would be many more people on welfare and food stamps were it not for income from marijuana. Officials stage annual "Green Harvests" to track down and destroy the pot. They use helicopters to spot large plots, which are usually on publicly owned or plantation lands so as to make it more difficult to trace ownership.

"The pot grower photographed, who obviously can't be identified or located except as being on Kauai, had about 30 mature plants and about 100 seedlings in an area behind his home. The 100 seedlings, he said, would produce several thousand dollars worth of pot."

—from the notes of photographer
Kent Kobersteen

• *Above*

An inmate at the Oahu Community Corrections Center, flashes the "shakka" sign with his extended thumb and little finger, a casual, wordless communication which means that everything is cool.

The main building at OCCC, Hawaii's largest prison, is a recently built collection of modules interspersed with small recreation gardens. Each module houses 30 inmates who live, work and eat as a group, an arrangement that effectively controls power-cliques among the inmates and, at the same time, encourages a sense of group responsibility within the modules.

Overcrowding at OCCC has forced the use of two older wings of the prison, where this photo was taken.

Photographer:
Paul Chesley

• *Right*

A triggerfish off Molokini, a tiny volcanic islet off the coast of Maui.

Photographer:
David Doubilet

• *Left*

A surfer jams beneath the cloudlike turbulence of a breaking Sunset Beach wave.

Photographer:
Wayne Levin

• *Above*

A spotface hawkfish, a second-rate swimmer and one of the laziest feeders in Hawaiian waters, waits for lunch to swim by its perch in the reef off Molokini.

Photographer:
David Doubilet

• *Following page*

Watching surfers ride the big waves on the North Shore.

Photographer:
Robin Moyer

Robin Moyer

• *Left*

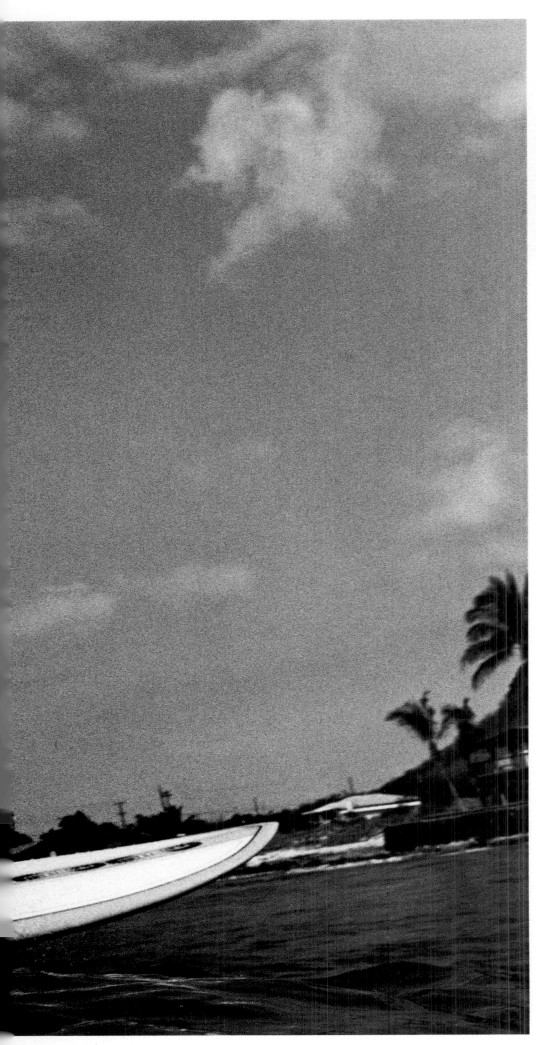

Teamwork on Waimea Bay.
Photographer:
Wayne Levin

• *Above*

Surfing life: Australian surfers Gary "Kong" Elkerton, Chappy Jennings and Bryce Ellis share an apartment on the North Shore during the winter series of ASP (Association of Surfing Professionals) contests in Hawaii. A year of professional surfing includes stops in Florida, New Jersey, Brazil, South Africa, California and Australia.
Photographer:
Aaron Chang

• *Left*

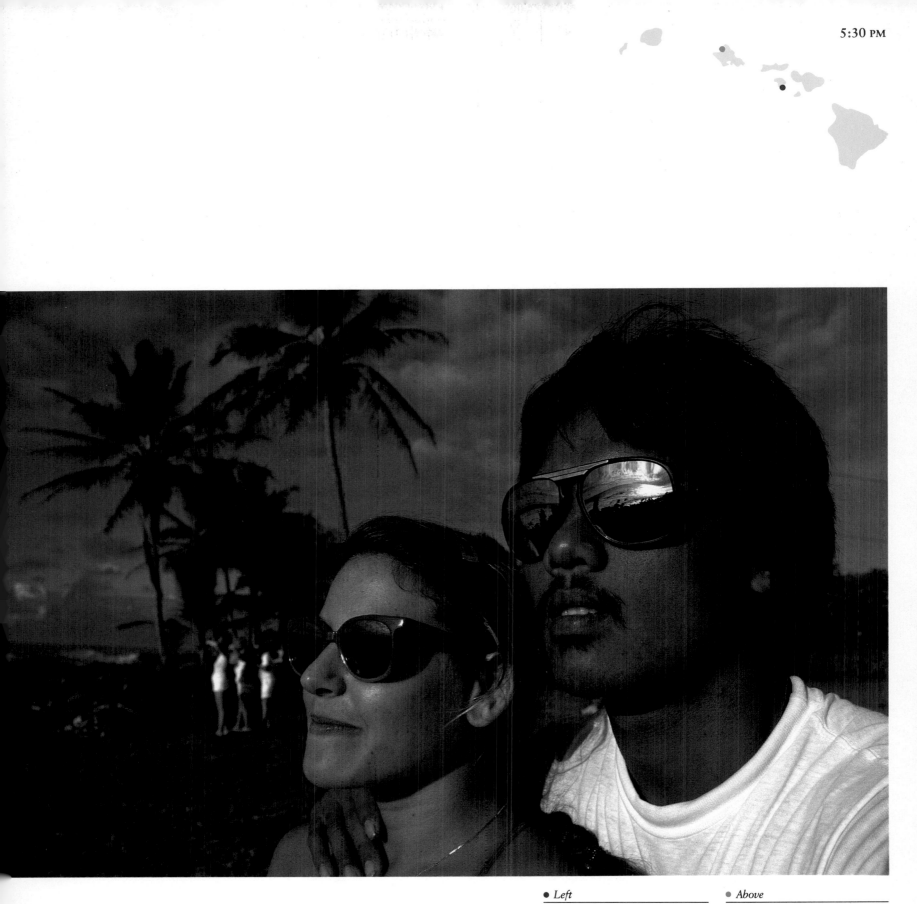

Spear fisherman, Pu'u Pehe Cove, Lanai.

Photographer:
Rich Clarkson

• *Above*

Waimea Bay, Oahu.

Photographer:
Matthew Naythons

• *Above, left*

After work it's pau hana time at the Koloa Broiler in funky Koloa, Kauai.

Photographer:
Douglas Kirkland

• *Above, right*

The Kona Inn Bar on the Big Island.

Photographer:
Star Black

• *Right*

Lori Ornellos, owner of the 50th State Bar, "The Friendliest Place in Hilo."

Photographer:
William Albert Allard

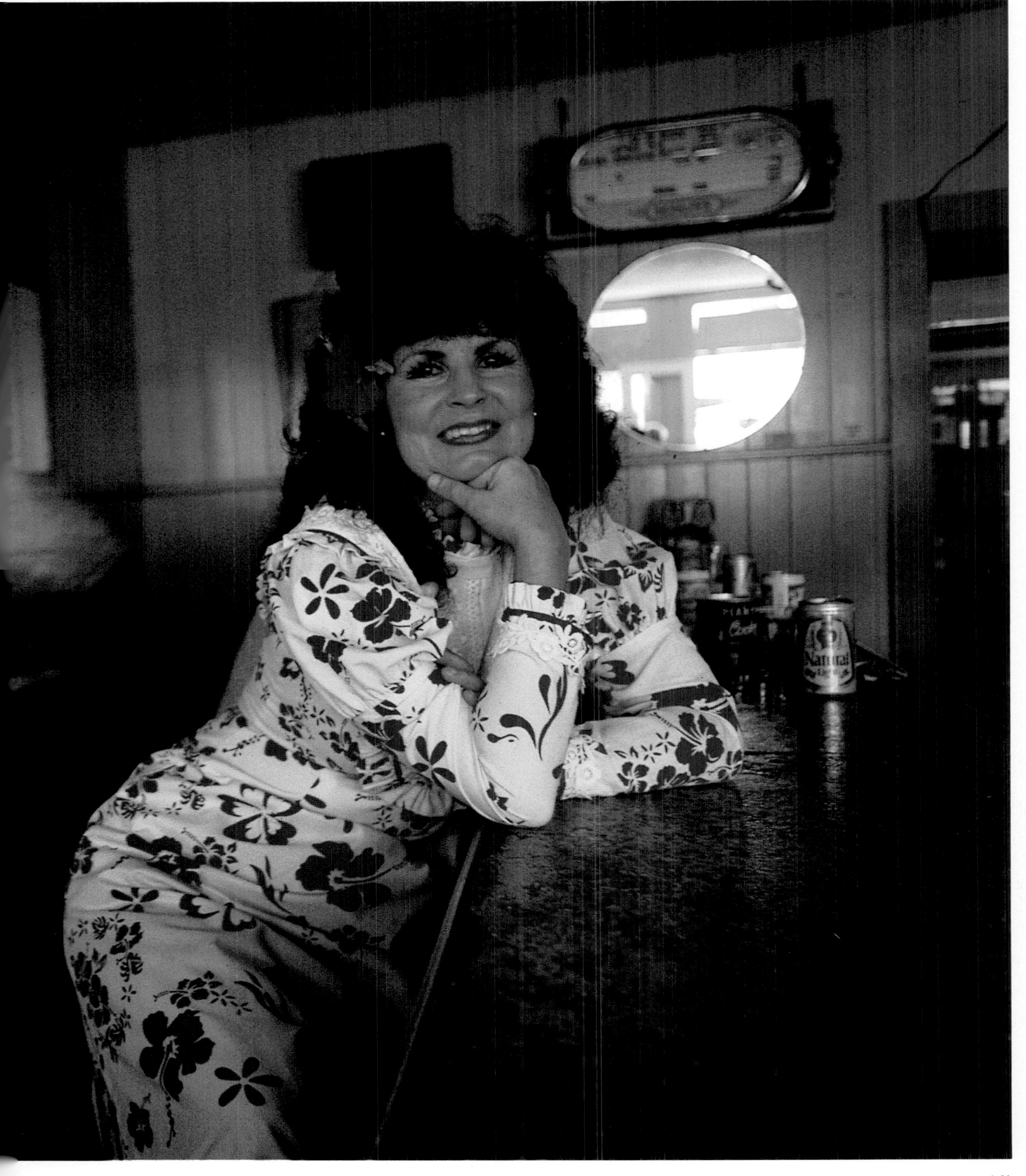

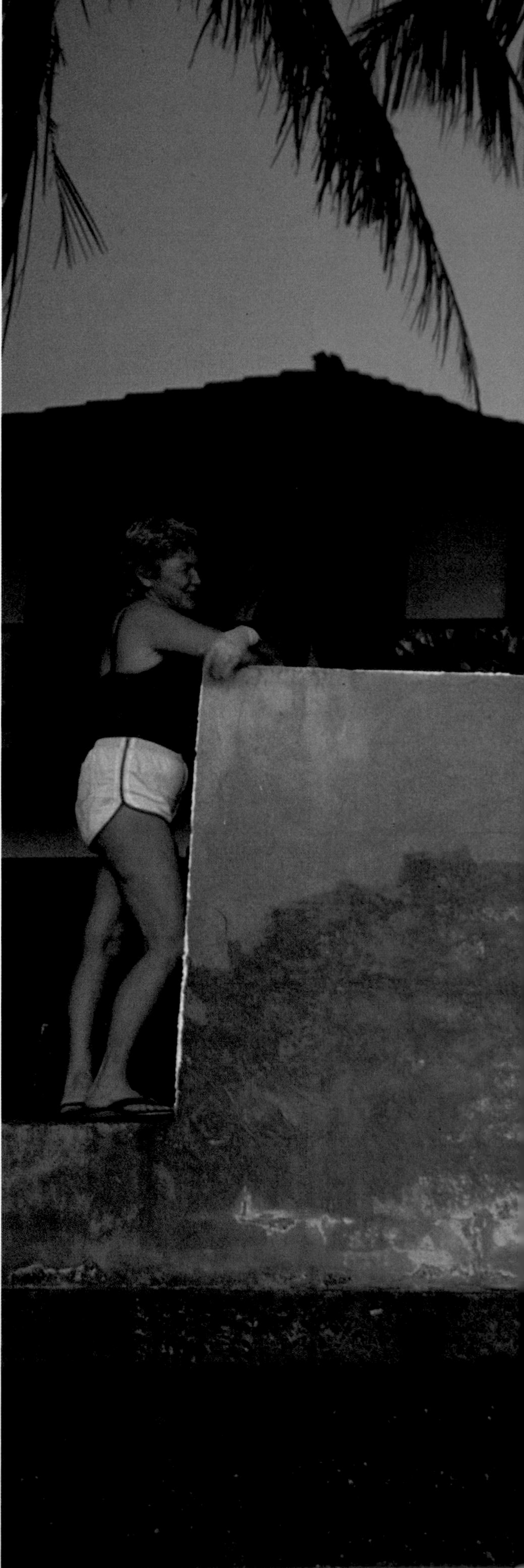

• *Above*

Good friends Ui'ilani Akao and Mahealani Kam visit through the glass doors of McInerny's in Waikiki.

Photographer:
Gerd Ludwig

• *Right*

Neighbors Pegi Scully and Marta Sanburn chat on the sea wall at Portlock, an old beach community whose waterfront shacks have been remodeled into million-dollar mini-estates.

Photographer:
David Alan Harvey

HONOLU
CLUB

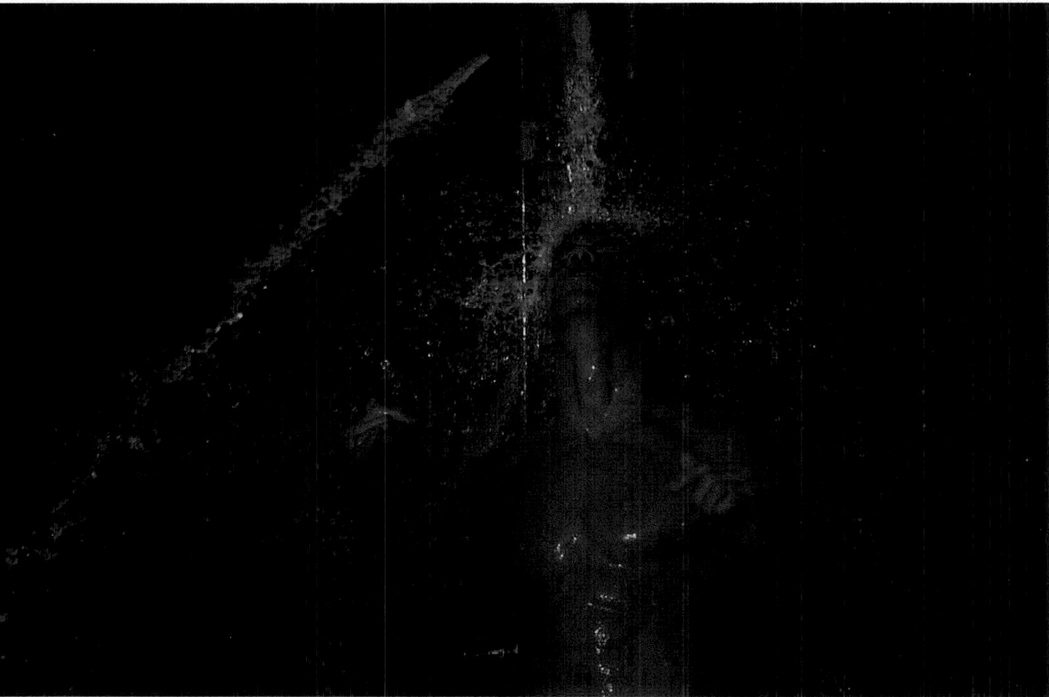

Left

The setting sun dances on the waters off Waikiki.

Photographer:

Gordon Parks

Above

Getting the salt off after surfing at Sandy Beach. Surfing is a popular extracurricular activity for Oahu's high-school students.

Photographer:

David Alan Harvey

Following page

World famous, seen by millions, different every night: a show-stopping sunset at Waikiki.

Photographer:

Alon Reininger

Alon Reininger

Just before sunset on December 2, *A Day in the Life of Hawaii* editor David Cohen decided to march down to Waikiki Beach and take a few snapshots with his Kodamatic instant camera. As the light slowly faded, he invited anyone walking by to jump up in the air while he snapped their pictures.

Dan Dry

Jean-Pierre Laffont

대한민국해군
대한민국해군

Mark S. Wexler

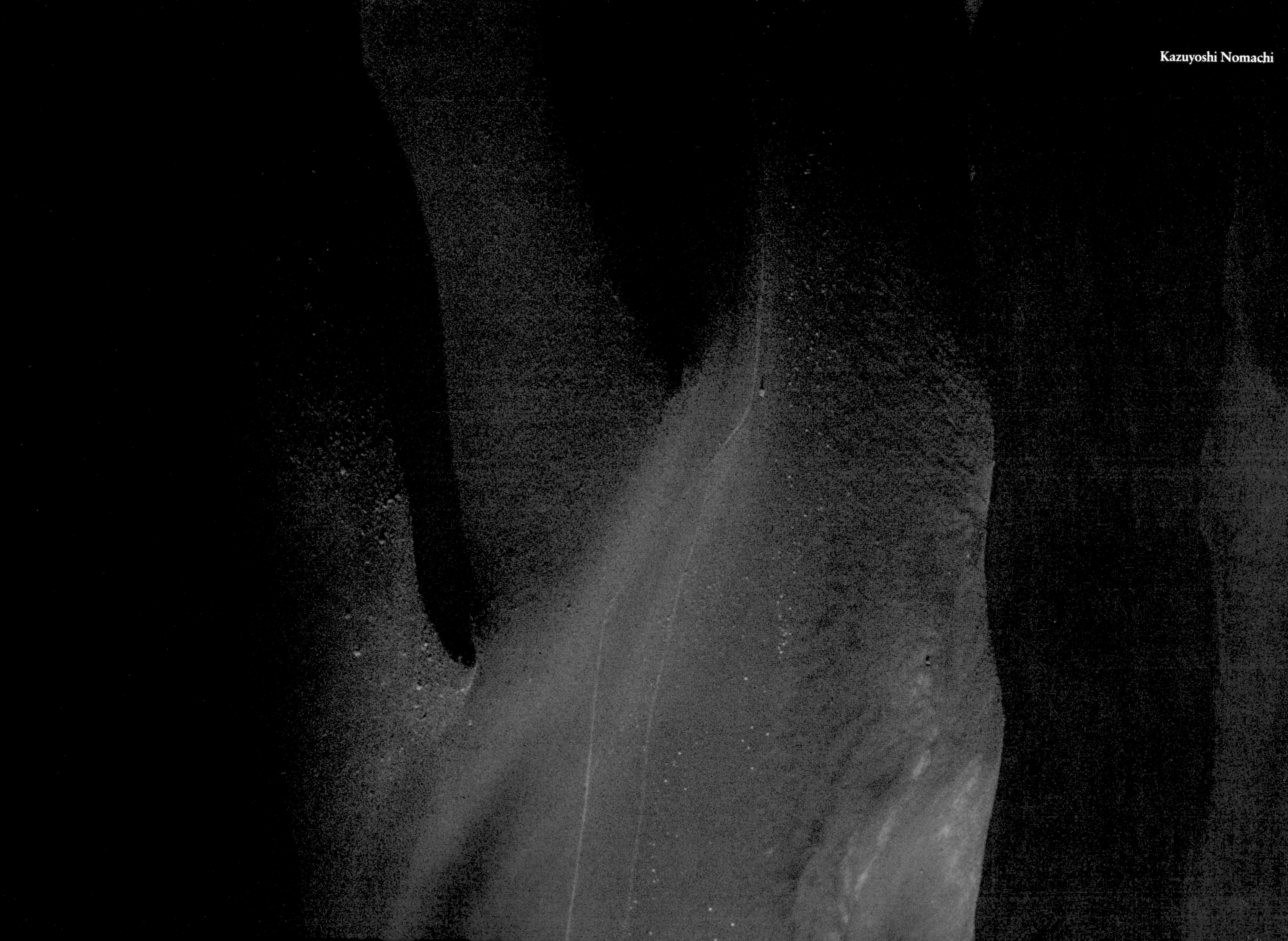

Kazuyoshi Nomachi

Paul Chesley

ISHADO
ARAKAWA
比嘉家之墓
HIGA
高森家之墓
TAKAMORI

Matthew Naythons

Previous pages 172–173
At Kaunakakai on Molokai, members of Moana's Polynesian Troupe rehearse for their Christmas performances.
Photographer:
Dan Dry

Previous pages 174–175
Korean sailors on shore leave stop at the Pali Lookout, where Honolulu's lush Nuuanu Valley suddenly drops away to a view of the Windward Side.
Photographer:
Jean-Pierre Laffont

Previous pages 176–177
"I've been doing a man's work all my life," says Anna Lindsey Perry-Fiske, owner of Anna Ranch in the lush cowtown of Waimea on the Big Island. A flamboyant figure in island society and a respected fund-raiser, Perry-Fiske rode in the 1972 Rose Bowl Parade as "Queen of Hawaii."
Photographer:
Mark S. Wexler

Previous pages 178–179
The setting sun lingers on cinder cones inside Haleakala Crater, a huge erosional depression at the summit of the dormant volcano. Haleakala (House of the Sun) rises 10,000 feet from sea level on Maui.
Photographer:
Kazuyoshi Nomachi

Previous pages 180–181
A Japanese cemetery in Nuuanu Valley, Honolulu.
Photographer:
Paul Chesley

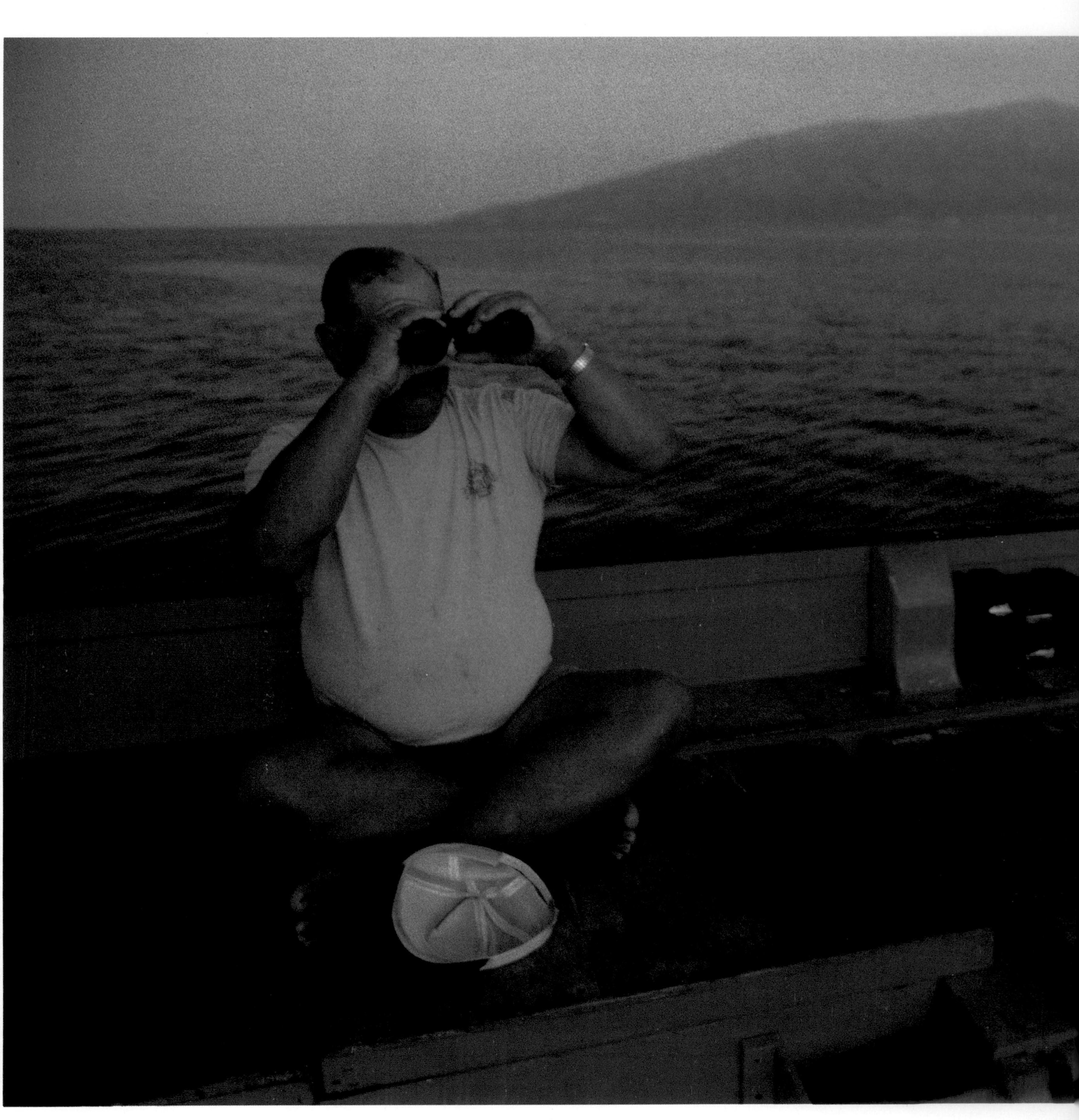

Previous pages 182–183
Paul Ogasawara, owner of Paul's Repair, a service station in Pahoa, Hawaii. The crosses are shadows cast by car jack handles.
Photographer:
Matthew Naythons

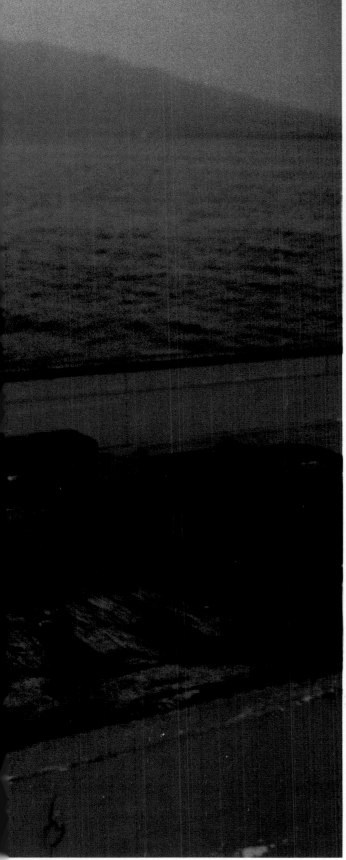

Left
Fisherman Sonny Bal off the coast of Maui.
Photographer:
Stephanie Maze

Above
The lava cross atop Lyon's Hill in Hana is a memorial to Paul Fagan, who, in the late 1940s, established Hana Ranch and built the Hotel Hana Maui. Fagan's hotel brought a steady stream of discriminating, wealthy travelers to the small, isolated town, often referred to as "Heavenly Hana."
Photographer:
Michael O'Brien

Left

Torch fisherman George Ota hunts for squid and octopus on the shallow reef off the coast of Koko Head, Oahu. His headgear is an improvement on the old hand-held torches used by Hawaiian fishermen to attract reef fish at night.

Photographer:
David Alan Harvey

Above

he PRI refinery at Campbell dustrial Park, Oahu.

otographer:
regory Heisler

Right

Born in Honolulu to Korean parents, Hi Shang Kim has been a cab driver for 25 years. This is his second decorated taxi.

Photographer:
Paul Chesley

• *Below, left*

Artist Randy Hokushin "paints" clay vessels with smoke from carefully controlled fires at his studio in Pupukea, Oahu. Hokushin has studied this ancient Japanese technique for ten years.

Photographer:
Aaron Chang

• *Below, right*

Pegge Hopper, a well-known local painter, works on a mural for Honolulu International Airport.

Photographer:
Dana Fineman

• *Following page*

Singers in a Christmas pageant at the Neil Blaisdell Center, Honolulu.

Photographer:
Rick Smolan

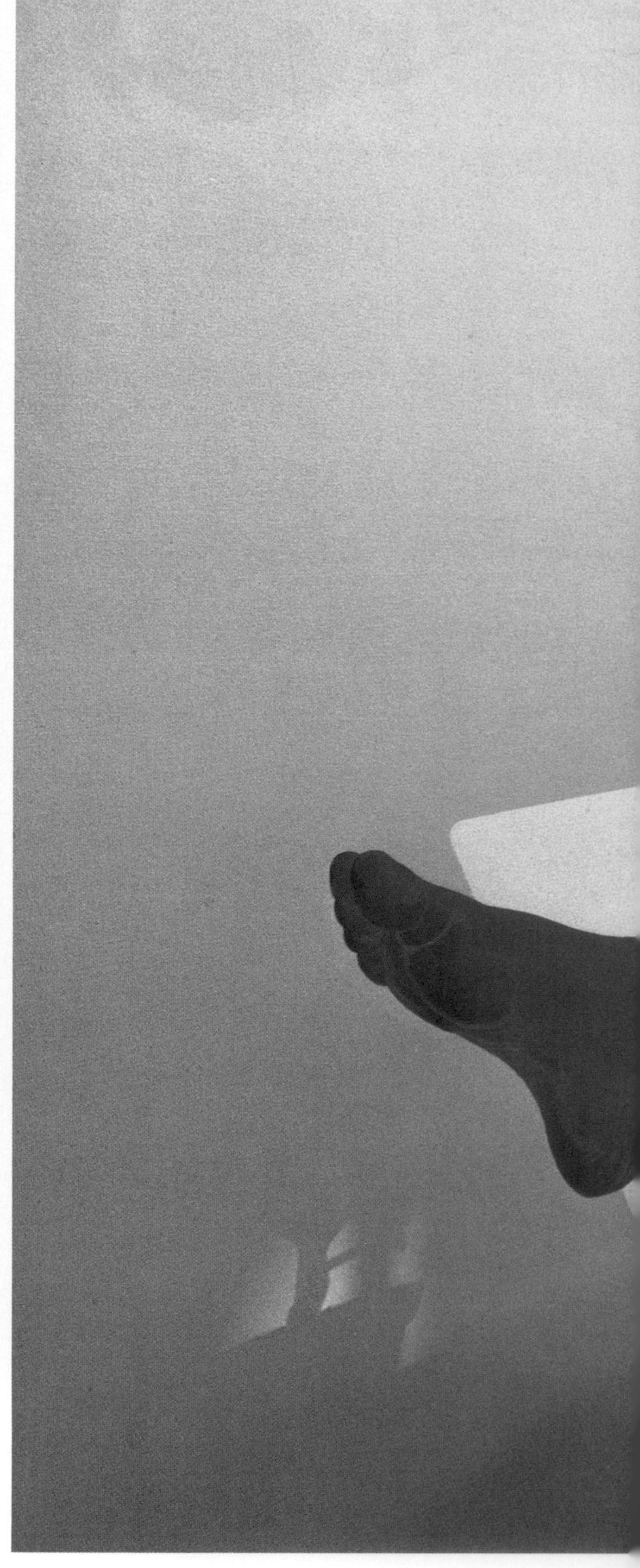

Rick Smolan

Left

In the winning football team's locker room at Aloha Stadium, minutes after the West beat the East in the Oahu Interscholastic League All-Star Game, 11-8.
Photographer:
Gregory Heisler

Above

One-on-one at the Koloa Recreation Center, Kauai.
Photographer:
Ken Sakamoto

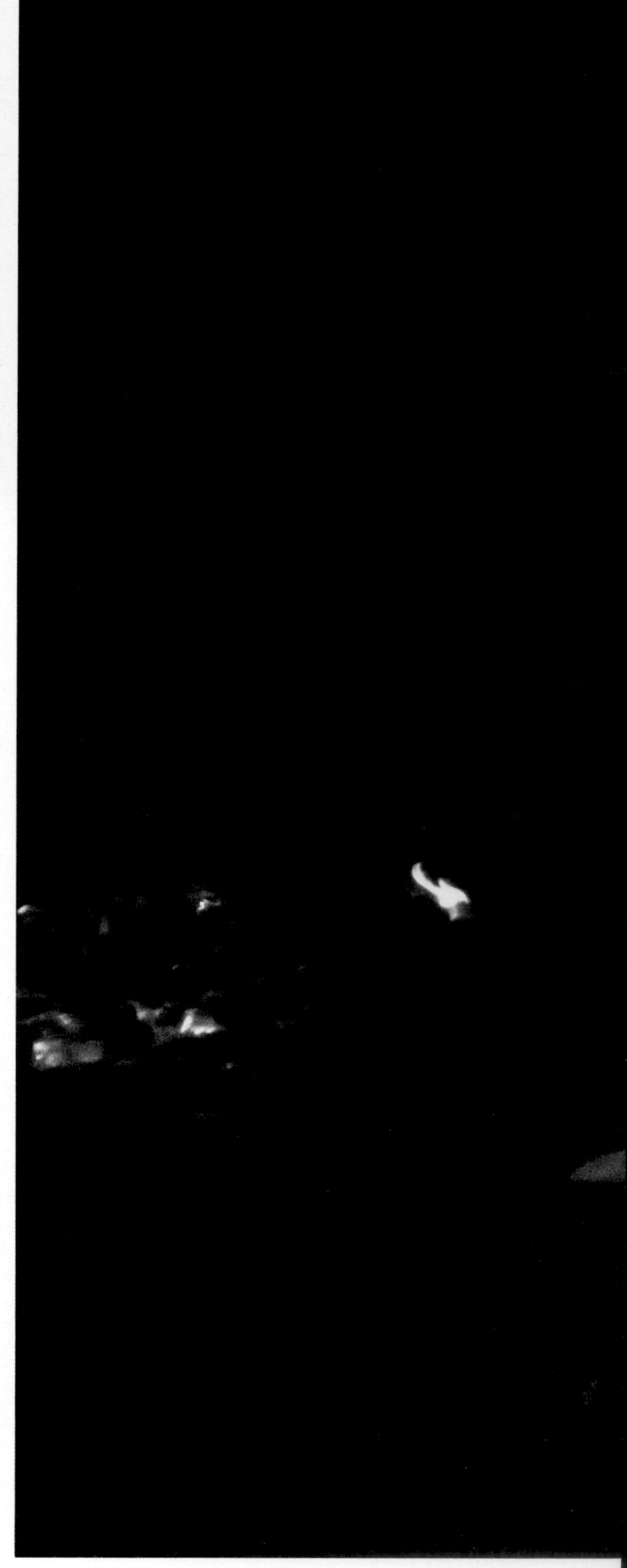

• *Above*

Farmer's meal, Hana, Maui.
Photographer:
Michael O'Brien

• *Right*

Preparations for a luau at the home of Joe Lapilio in Waianae, Oahu. Friends and family help prepare three 300-pound pigs for roasting in a traditional Hawaiian imu, an earthen pit lined with stones and fueled with kiawe wood.
Photographer:
Arthur Grace

• *Above*

Ten minutes till curtain at Seabury Hall, a boarding school on Maui. Tonight's presentation: Kurt Weil's "Threepenny Opera."

Photographer:
Stephanie Maze

• *Right*

Nalini Almazan, a contestant in the Kauai Junior Miss Pageant, crosses the runway during a full-dress rehearsal in Lihue. The next evening, Almazan was named first runner-up.

Photographer:
Jay Maisel

• *Following page*

Helene Kuuleimano Kahaunaele, Miss Kauai 1983. She is Hawaiian-Norwegian-Japanese-Spanish-English-German-Irish. In this sense, she is typically Hawaiian.

Photographer:
Dirck Halstead

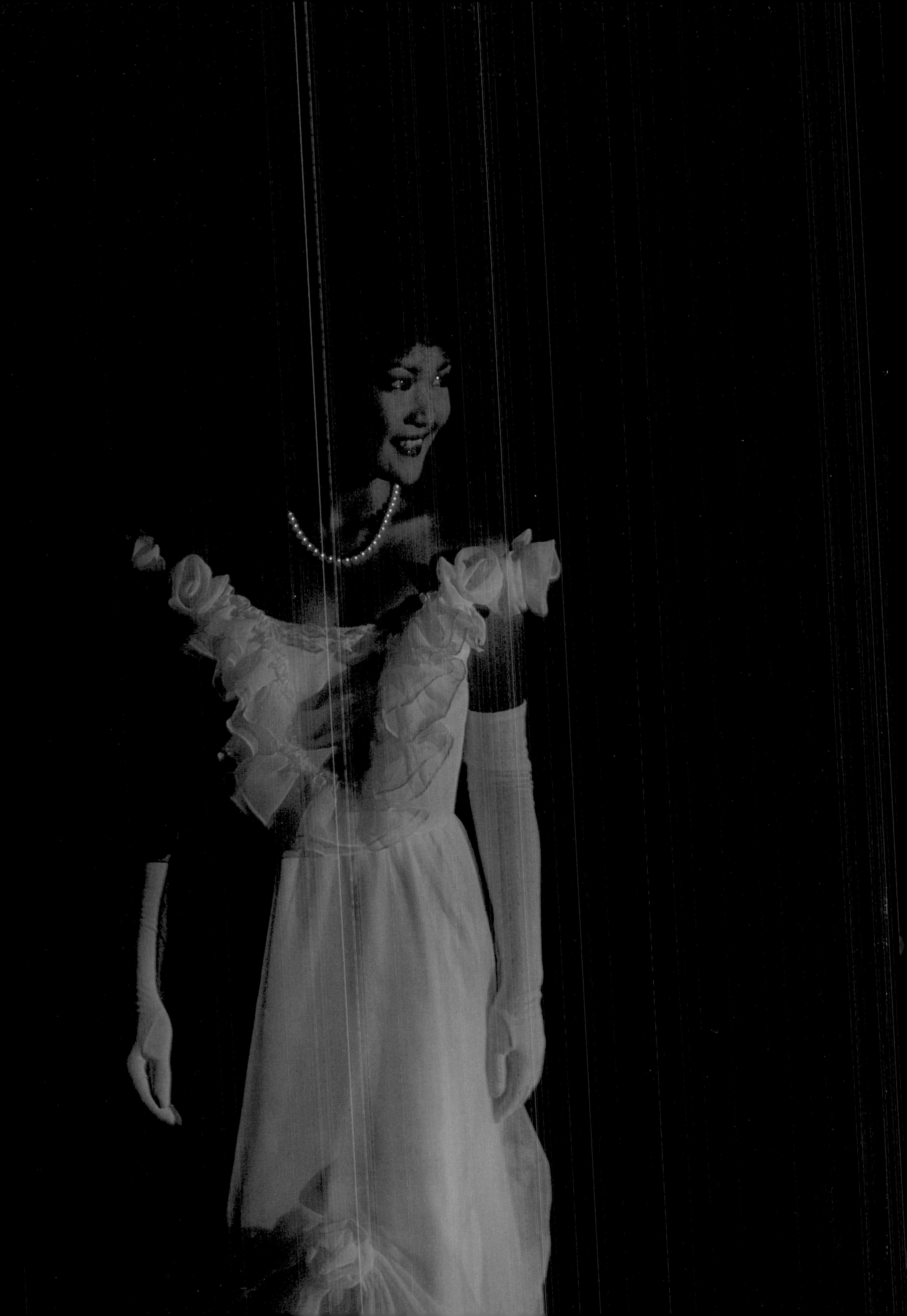

L.A. photographer Dana Fineman set up her cameras and lights outside The Wave, a Waikiki club where locals, haoles, tourists, gays, soldiers, sailors, occasional celebrities and die-hard trendies meet for late-night dance music.

Dancer Cindy Lutz.

Students Anne Miyashiro, Billi M. Shackley and Julie Chung.

Sonya Mendez, lead singer of Sonya & Revolución.

Marcelo Kimlaborte, apprentice pastry cook.

• *Above*

As December 2 ended, three-year-old Lorca Lueras may have been dreaming of Ewoks.

Photographer:
Leonard Lueras

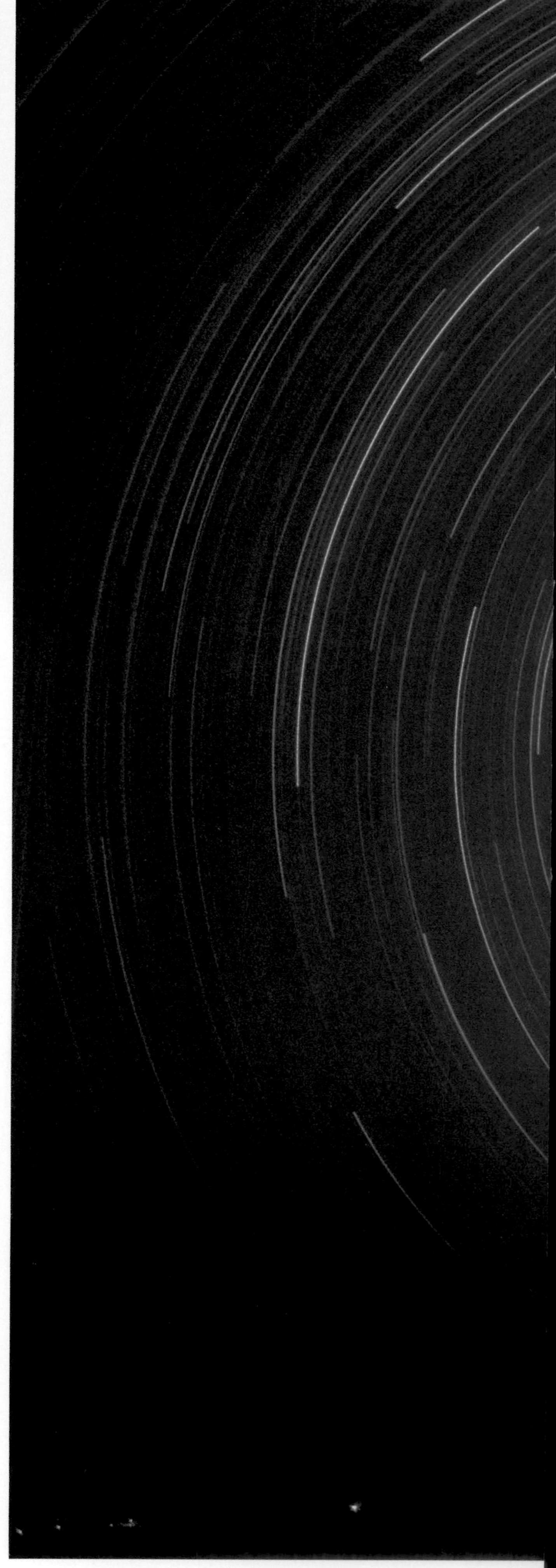

• *Right*

On a clear night at 13,700 feet, a streak of red car lights followed the midnight shift of scientists into Mauna Kea Observatory. This time-exposure photograph was made from 7:30 PM to midnight on December 2. As the earth rotates, the stars above Hawaii seem to wheel around stationary Polaris, the North Star, which guided the first adventurers to Hawaii.

Photographer:
Shelly Katz

• *Below, left*

Backstage at Club Hubba Hubba on Hotel Street, the main drag of downtown Honolulu's faded red-light district.

Photographer:
P. F. Bentley

• *Below, right*

Sailors on shore leave from two Korean destroyers try to bridge the language gap.

Photographer:
Paul Chesley

• *Bottom, right*

Chinatown, just before midnight.

Photographer:
Leonard Lueras

• *Following page*

Gossip and good manners at 3D, a punk-rock club in Honolulu.

Photographer:
Donna Ferrato

RLS
VE STAGE SHOW
ESQUIRE

Donna Ferrato

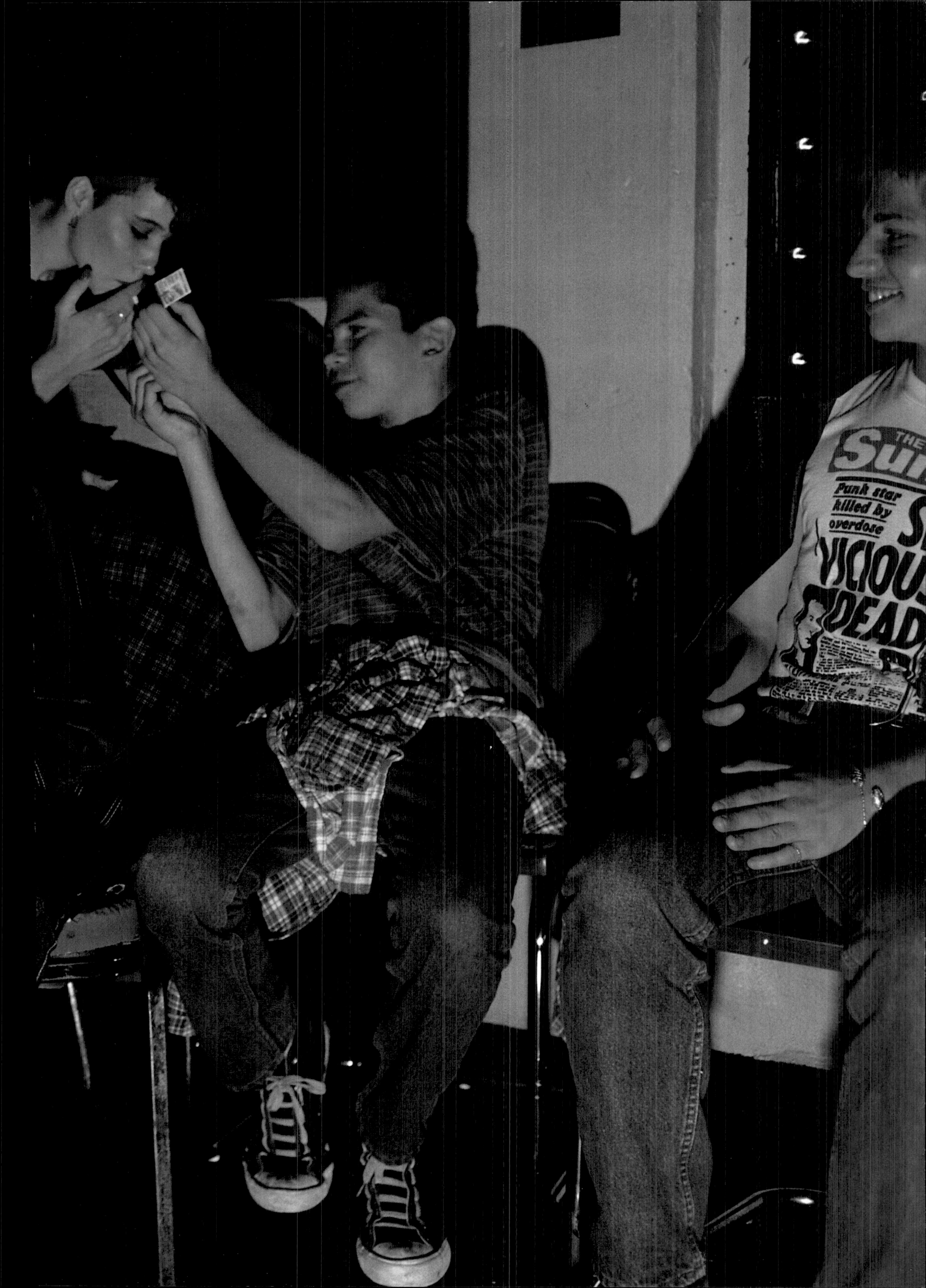
Punk star
killed by
overdose

• *Below, left*

Just after closing time, old friends gather at Bullocks Restaurant, perched 1,500 feet up the slopes of Haleakala, on Maui. Police Sergeant Paul Winters (right) and his wife, Faith, Patrolman Wayne Ribao, Elvin Rodrigues and Bullocks owner Paul Elkins share a few moments together before heading home.
Photographer:
Robin Moyer

• *Below*

Dancers with Tihati's Polynesian Revue change costume after the last show at Waikiki's Moana Hotel.
Photographer:
Gerd Ludwig

• *Following page*

An open-shutter zoom catches the razzmatazz of Honolulu on a Friday night.
Photographer:
Jean-Pierre Laffont

• *Above*

Photographer Gregory Heisler's last stop of the day was Castle Park, west of Honolulu. Heisler says, "I'm walking through this deserted amusement park and I pass a video arcade. I hate video games so I decided I absolutely wasn't going to shoot that. All of a sudden ten local kids push by me and rush into the arcade and they start break dancing on the floor. The kids look like they're mounted on ball bearings or bee's wax or something. They're whizzing around like they have teflon hands, just flying around the floor, doing handstands. They're going like ten feet in the air and landing directly on their skulls. It was so dark, I couldn't even see. I honestly don't know if the pictures are even in focus."
Photographer:
Gregory Heisler

Jean-Pierre Laffont

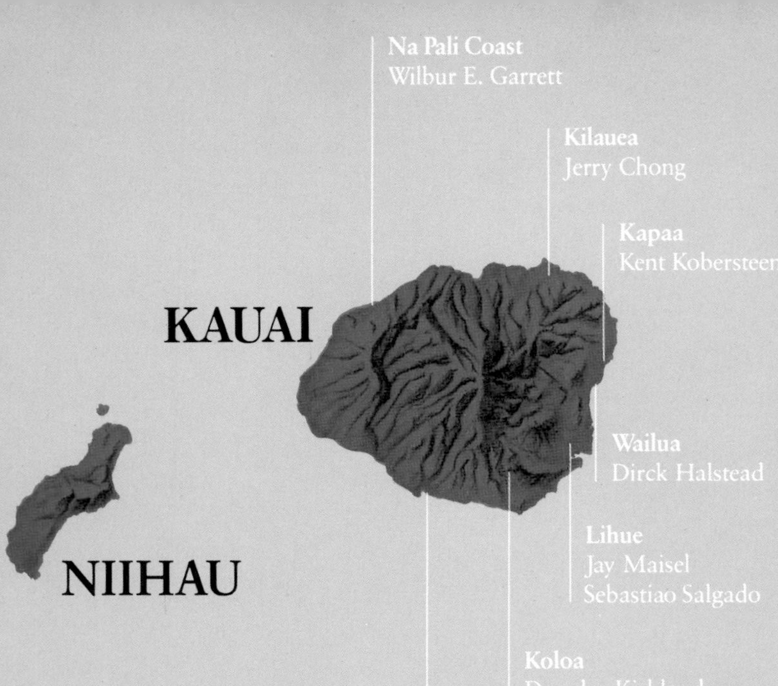

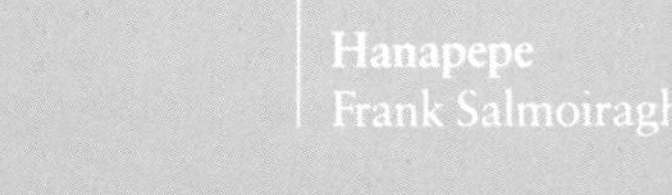

JERRY CHONG

7:00 AM
Harvesting guava fruit at Kilauea Agronomics on Kauai's north shore.

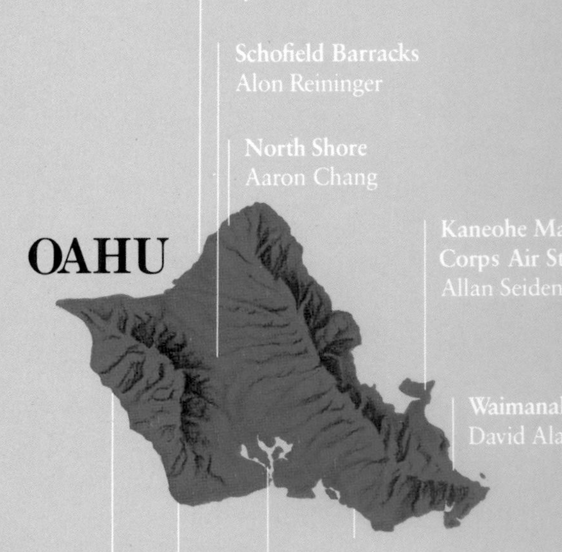

RITA GORMLEY

6:30 AM
The heights of Mauna Kea reflected in a small pond outside of Hilo, Hawaii.

ABBAS

2:00 PM
A Samoan gentleman in a sarong pauses from work on his car in suburban Honolulu, Oahu.

ELLIOTT ERWITT

1:00 PM
Tourists frolicking for the camera in Waikiki, Oahu.

SABRA McCRACKEN

12:30 PM
Traditional hula at Hilo, Hawaii.

RON JETT

8:30 AM
Ranger Julie Shackelton and her horse Kukui in Volcanoes National Park, Hawaii.

CLIFF HOLLENBECK

3:00 PM
Sister Wilma has spent thirty years administering medical aid to the residents of the leper colony at Kalaupapa, Molokai.

FRANK FOURNIER

1:30 PM
A catamaran ride off Kawaihae, Hawaii.

NEAL ULEVICH

5:00 PM
Richard Tong and Hawaii's uncommonly common rainbow in Hilo, Hawaii.

EDDIE ADAMS

8:00 AM
Parker Ranch cowboys select their horses for the day's work on the island of Hawaii.

KAZUYOSHI NOMACHI

8:00 AM
Haleakala Crater, Maui.

SHOMEI TOMATSU

11:00 AM
Aquarobics at the YWCA in Honolulu, Oahu.

A Day in the Life Revisited

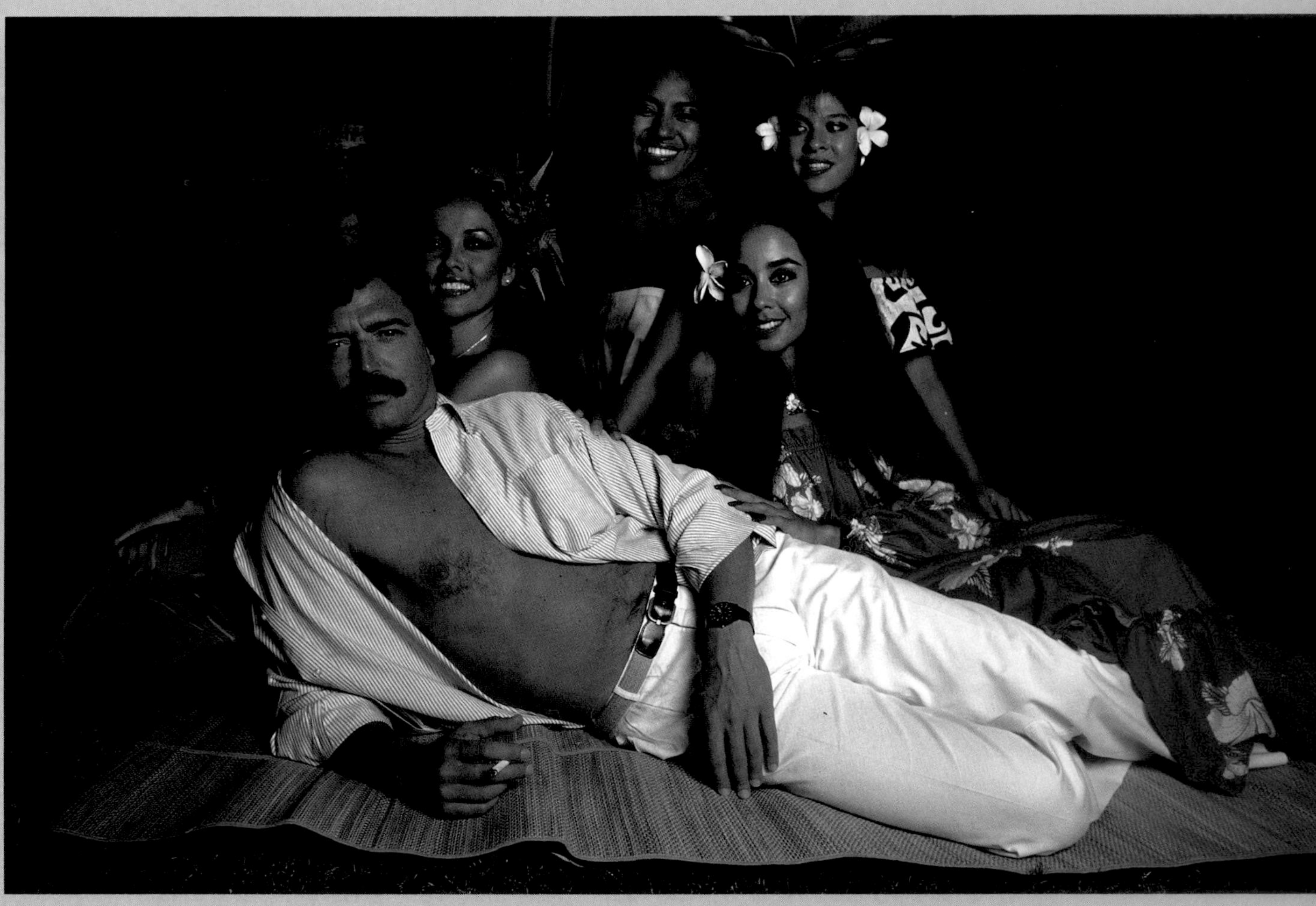

***Time* magazine photographer Arthur Grace and friends at a real Hawaiian luau.**

On December 2, 1983, fifty of the world's top photojournalists descended on Hawaii for a remarkable project that, in its budget, cast, and organization, more closely resembled the making of a feature film than a book. For one twenty-four-hour period they would search out and shoot the best and worst of "paradise" to make a unique pictorial book, *A Day in the Life of Hawaii (DITLOHA),* and time the publication to coincide with Hawaii's Silver Jubilee of statehood.

Hawaii is a state where urban sprawl encroaches on majestic mountains, where farm hands still whisper the names of the big plantation owners, where every conceivable ethnic mix lives side-by-side in relative harmony. Hawaii is also a state where tourism is the number-one business, with defense, marijuana, sugar cane and pineapples competitive seconds.

"A Day in the Life of America," a photo-essay issue for *Life* magazine back in 1974, employed a hundred photographers. Among them was Rick Smolan, an internationally known photographer who had covered major stories for prestigious publications throughout the world.

In 1981, David Cohen, a former director and managing editor of Contact Press Images, joined Smolan and his team to put together *A Day in the Life of Australia.* They believed that the public would be interested in an honest look at a place by an international group of journalists who told their stories with their cameras. It was a risk that publishers were not willing to accept. Every publisher they approached said the idea would never work.

But Smolan's friends encouraged him. "Every time I mentioned *Day in the Life* to a photographer, I would see a spark in their eyes at the craziness of the idea. It was the enthusiasm of the photographers that made us decide to ignore the experts and figure out a way to do it. The whole thing became an obsession. We borrowed money from everyone—families, corporations, girl friends—you name it."

The experts waited for them to fall on their faces. Instead, the risk paid off. The Australia book was covered in *Time, Life,* and *Newsweek* and featured on television shows around the world. It has gone on to become one of the best-selling picture books in recent years, having already sold 180,000 copies internationally.

In August, 1983, Smolan and Cohen were approached by a public relations firm in Hawaii. Sheila Donnelly, who represents Stryker Weiner Associates, said, "Hawaii isn't just girls in hula skirts, or tourists in matching muumuus and aloha shirts. We're very proud of Hawaii." Within days Donnelly started working on logistics. "Everything starts with the beds. As soon as Sheraton gave us the beds, I knew we had a project." As with everyone else involved with *DITLOHA,* her enthusiasm never wavered. "We all willed it to happen."

Working backward from the publication date, Smolan and Cohen set up their timetable. They were left with only three weeks to raise the $600,000 it would take just to get the project off the ground. "Ordinarily," says Cohen, "three weeks would not be enough time to raise that sort of money, but these projects have a strange serendipitous nature. Whenever we were in the most trouble, someone with the right skills showed up and saved the day. In this case, it was Walter Dods." Within a matter of days, Dods, Vice President of First Hawaiian Bank, organized an informal consortium of Hawaii's leading businesses to support the project. Dods explained the unusual ground rules to the companies as well—unlike most ventures, the investors would have no control over the final product.

The underwriters agreed and by the end of the three-week period, First Hawaiian Bank, Duty Free Shoppers, Matson Navigation, Hawaiian Telephone, Pacific Resources, Inc., the Hawaii Visitors Bureau, and the Department of Planning and Economic Development had chipped in $50,000 apiece. United Airlines had donated all first-class airfares. Aloha Airlines had guaranteed all inter-island flights. Sheraton Hotels had given a thousand nights-worth of rooms. The accounting firm of Coopers & Lybrand offered to do the project's accounting, gratis. Wang Laboratories had donated a complete office system. Apple had sold them the new state-of-the-art LISA computer, at cost. Radio Shack had sold them fifty portable computers for the photographers at a tremendous discount. Holiday had donated rental cars. Kodak chipped in $50,000 worth of film and supplies, cameras for children, and prizes for the photo contest.

On October 5, Governor George Ariyoshi called a press conference at Washington Place, the governor's mansion, to announce the project to the state. Forty internationally known, award-winning photographers and ten local photographers would be put up for a week of seminars, briefings, computer training, the "big shoot," and debriefings. They would all waive their usual fees and receive a token $350, plus a free computer. The photographers would distribute Kodak disc cameras and film to school children. A page of the book would be allocated to the children's view of *DITLOHA;* another two pages would present the winners of the *Honolulu Advertiser*'s photo contest. The newspaper expected 5,000 entries. Thirty more Kodak cameras would go to the winners. The *Advertiser* was also set to do a pre-sale of the book. A local TV station, KGMB, volunteered to do twelve free commercials a day for six weeks. They would receive a percentage of the newspaper's profits, if there were any. Apparently, investors were interested in the project whether it turned a profit or not.

If all of this sounds like a bound-to-fail, hair-brained scheme, Cohen and Smolan decided to multiply the odds ten-fold. The book would be just the beginning, followed by a *DITLOHA* calendar, a traveling photography exhibit, and a one-hour documentary film.

The logistics were mind-boggling. A salaried staff of eight worked for two months inviting photographers, making reservations, researching locations, hiring twenty-four helicopters, and turning reams of paper into press kits, assignment books, a prospectus, and schedules.

The assignment logistics team put together topics for assignments. Cohen and Smolan then tried to match the requirements of each assignment with the skills of each photographer. "We knew their strengths and some had indicated their preferences for certain subjects," said Cohen. "In some cases we gave the photographers something they were good at. Other times we couldn't resist giving them just the opposite. The assignment became a chance for the photographer to view Hawaii with a fresh eye and to make extraordinary photographs of ordinary events."

Gordon Parks, the respected author/photographer/director (*Shaft, The Learning Tree*) headed up the video project, with top Hollywood photographer Douglas Kirkland serving as producer. Fifty-seven hours of tape would be edited down to one hour of photography in motion. Four of the five cameramen were still photographers, including two-time Pulitzer Prize-winning photographer Stanley Forman, Magazine Photographer of the Year David Burnett, and Kirkland. The funds for the documentary were raised separately, with Sony loaning $200,000 in video equipment.

Project directors David Cohen and Rick Smolan settle an administrative dispute.

CAROL PUTNAM *Palo Alto Weekly*

Burnett

When you get fifty good photographers like this in one place, all working in the same period of time, it's like having fifty little test tubes, and you watch the little mice trying to crawl up the sides of the glass to do their best.

Halstead

I was assigned to shoot the "forbidden island"—Niihau. I knew I was in trouble when I heard that no one had ever been allowed to photograph on the island before. The last real outsider was a Japanese pilot who crashed there in 1941. He shot one of the islanders three times with a gun and, when he was caught, the islander picked him up and threw him against the wall and crushed him. So I knew I was in for trouble. . . .

It was suggested that I try to sneak onto the island. I never really thought of myself as the U.S. Marines or a one-man commando team, so the idea of a secret assault on an island where they crushed the last invader against the wall. . . . No, I decided I definitely wanted a formal invitation.

Adams

The high priestess gave me a lei and she said, "This is a lei of love, hold it in your hand." She took me by the arm and said, "Just place the lei on the altar and make a wish, anything dealing with love, or something you really want to happen." I did that, stepped back, and she put her arm on me. And I had the chills. It was just really nice.

Allard

Usually I photograph masculine subjects. I came to Hawaii hoping I could photograph something I don't normally do. Here I wanted to photograph women. If they were beautiful, that would be even better. Instead, they assigned me to a pig hunt.

The Day Before

The *DITLOHA* office, overlooking Waikiki Beach, becomes a center of frenetic activity. A photographer sits on the floor taking apart a piece of equipment, mumbling, "This had better work." *Time* magazine photographer Arthur Grace telephones a photolab, yelling that his test prints aren't back yet. A famous Japanese photographer refuses to go to the Big Island to shoot the erupting volcano—an assignment his colleagues have been begging for in an unseemly fashion. He didn't know until he arrived that he's afraid of volcanoes, and he won't even set foot on the island. In one corner a journalist tries to arrange to tag along with one of the photographers on the big day. "I'm going out to spend time with a three-hundred-pound Samoan surfer who lives in a tent with his wife and seven kids. I barely got him to let me photograph him. I can't be responsible for you, too. Forget it!"

Smolan and Cohen divide their time between smoothing ruffled feathers (the photojournalist—a strange species that lives most of the year out of a suitcase—has an ego that won't quit, a vocabulary that's heavy on profanity, a sense of adventure combined with artistic sensibility, and a need to be constantly reassured) and answering questions. "Why can't I have a helicopter? How do I change my flight? So-and-so says I can't shoot them, what now?" Smolan and Cohen slip away for a quick lunch.

A guy from the office comes by, his brow furrowed by worry. The forecast says rain. After months of planning, the whole book might end up as pictures of Hawaii in a tropical storm—and there's nothing to be done about it. Later that evening the gang is found on the roof of the Sheraton doing a traditional anti-rain dance and setting out a jigger of gin and a ti leaf to bring good weather. On the news that night it is reported that Kilauea volcano on the island of Hawaii is erupting with lava fountains spurting 400 feet in the air. Everyone wonders if it will continue into "The Day."

As the midnight hour looms closer, Cohen says, "Most of the time there's a very good working relationship between Rick and me, except for earlier today when I was seriously considering homicide. He comes up with these crazy ideas and he starts spinning them out. He creates a cyclone of more and more things that need to be done to make the idea work. Rick needs someone to control and channel his energy, because sometimes when he's just blasting off, it doesn't translate into a smooth operation. I never thought of myself as being tremendously organized but, compared to Rick, I am. And the more frightened he gets, the calmer he looks."

"The whole thing is on automatic," Smolan opines serenely. "Either this will work or it won't, but it's no longer in our control."

RICK SMOLAN

Eli Reed of Magnum, with Sheila Donnelly.

MAGGIE STEBER courtesy Eastman Kodak

Portable Radio Shack computers confuse Arnaud de Wildenberg of France and Gerd Ludwig of West German

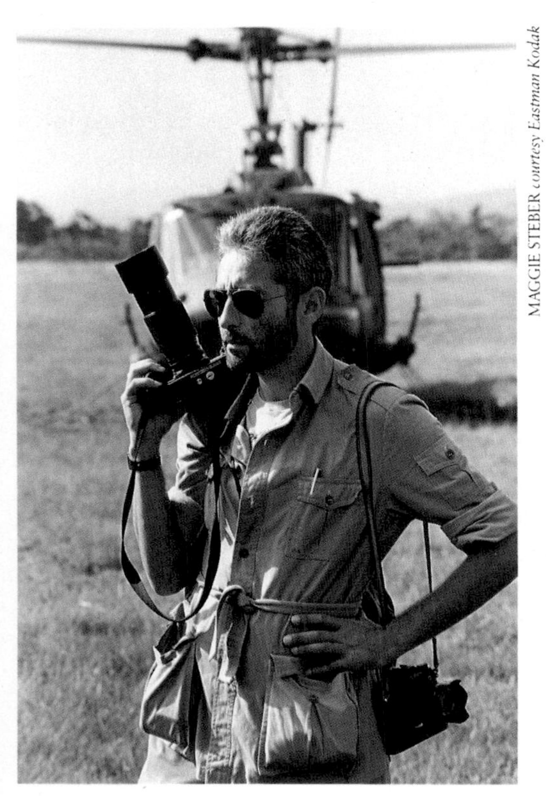

MAGGIE STEBER *courtesy Eastman Kodak*

Israeli photojournalist Alon Reininger with the Army at Schofield Barracks.

The Day

The purpose—to make a great book. The problem—it can't be just another pretty picture book. The purpose—to take great photos. The problem—to overcome obstacles in the forms of light, weather, equipment failure, reluctant subjects.

The gin must have worked. The weather is terrific except for the "vog"—volcanic haze. Within minutes after midnight, the photographers' fears and grumblings about "just another tourist promotion for Hawaii" are assuaged—due partly to the intricacy and planning of assignments (the advance publicity on the project itself, which has made almost everyone on the islands at least vaguely aware of *DITLOHA*'s minions and eager to participate at any level) and partly to the plain luck of some photographers, who stumble by accident onto the right place at the right time.

In a hospital room, right after midnight, a woman is in labor. The medical staff and the prospective father and mother ignore *National Geographic* photographer Jodi Cobb as she records the birth, as well as the video crew, which is shooting Cobb. "Everyone else has done a lot more to be at this place than I have," says Jodi Cobb, whose assignment it is to photograph "a birth, a death, and a wedding—the significant events of life." This first segment of Cobb's day ends when the mother receives the child in her arms and utters her first words to him, "Well, I guess we've got to give you a name now, boy."

"My day started off miserably," says Donna Ferrato, who spends the midnight hours covering a Waikiki nightclub. "All of my equipment broke down and the time was ticking away. It was 12:45 AM. Everyone else was getting great shots. A friend pulled me outside, calmed me down, and helped me get my things together. I was also assigned Diamond Head crater. I hate mountain climbing. I'm *not* Ansel Adams! Then I found the janitor of Diamond Head and he showed me how dirty it is up there. I mean, old junked washing machines falling off Diamond Head! Now I think I have pneumonia. I'm about ready to die. . . ."

Japanese photographer Shomei Tomatsu moves like a chameleon, almost disappearing into the woodwork of a Filipino pool hall. Earlier in the day he had photographed privileged children at an exclusive school and their opposite number at the Office of Children and Youth, where smears of fingerprint ink decorate the institutional-green walls. In all three places people have heard of *DITLOHA*. Through an interpreter, he says, "I want to show how the rich, middle and poor classes live in one day." There's a Japanese word for Tomatsu's quest, which roughly translates "the reek of the human." Throughout the twenty-four hours, efforts are made for Tomatsu to take pictures of a particular well-to-do Hawaiian, but his wife won't let anyone in the house. The person in charge of setting this up grumbles, "His wife is known throughout the state as a very difficult woman."

"Stop the car! That's it!" yells Carl Ganter, at eighteen the youngest photographer. It's getting close to midnight and he's determined to stay up for the full twenty-four hours. He's been dozing while being chauffeured up and down the Oahu coast. (He couldn't rent his own car—too young.) But now he sees his dream picture before him, a United States Coast Guard cutter balanced majestically between two metal walls in dry dock. The whole area is lit up bright as high noon. A gigantic sand blaster fills the area with flecks of paint from the ship's hull and a racket that makes the body quiver. Ganter,

ROBIN MOYER

David Burnett working on the documentary in Maui's cowboy country.

Katz

I was on top of the Mauna Kea Observatory at fourteen thousand feet. Temperatures were in the teens and twentys. I thought I was coming to Hawaii and I ended up in the Arctic. The second night I was there the winds were over 90 knots. You don't move around in weather like that. Most of the time I was gasping for air. I felt a great affinity with David Doubilet working underwater. I know I took more oxygen than he did. The first 24 hours I was up there, I wouldn't walk out of the room if there wasn't an oxygen tank somewhere.

On the night of December 2, I was setting up my tripod to take a four-hour time exposure to show the stars swirling around the observatory as the earth rotated. I got out of the jeep, and a gust of wind suddenly ripped the door off the jeep, metal hinges and all. The door came flying right at me and knocked me down flat. I kissed the ground and for a couple of minutes I didn't think I was going to get up.

Naythons

The Pahoa Inn Cafe was this time capsule. There was a wonderful waitress named Goldie. She would be Alice in Alice's Restaurant. She was 29 years old—zaftig with golden red hair—smashing. She's lived in Hawaii for three or four years. Every now and then she would turn on this big smile and the whole room would warm up ten degrees.

Dana Fineman sets up a shot outside The Wave discotheque in Waikiki.

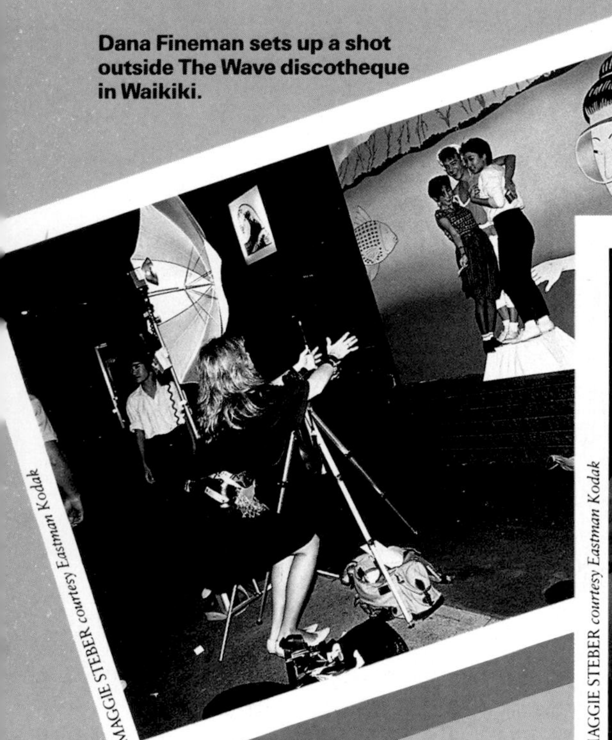

MAGGIE STEBER *courtesy Eastman Kodak*

MAGGIE STEBER *courtesy Eastman Kodak*

Time **magazine photographer Shelly Katz shows a new friend how to operate a Kodak disc camera.**

RICK SMOLAN

Documentary director Gordon Parks.

Maze

I got in the water with the proud fishermen and somehow managed to trip over the net and sink one of my cameras. It was ruined. At first I had been told that I was not allowed to go with them on the boat because there's a law of the sea, a superstition, that says that women bring bad luck to the fishermen. I convinced the captain that it was very important for me to go along. Eight hours after we headed out to sea, I understood that maybe superstition was not the real problem, but rather that they didn't have adequate toilet facilities for women on board.

two men from the ship in hard hats, the driver and a reporter (both women, both in heels) climb up a hundred feet—hand over hand—to a catwalk. After the ship has been photographed from every conceivable angle, the men in hard hats ask for souvenir prints for their ship's diary.

Jennifer Erwitt, *DITLOHA*'s production coordinator, wanders into a day-care center for handicapped people and meets Thomas, a young man in his twenties who was crippled in a car accident. He can barely speak and is incapable of using his hands to write. He pulls his shirt off to display the tattoos all over his body. One of the nurses watching the scene offers to take a Kodamatic picture of the two talking together, and Erwitt signs her name on the photograph. Thomas asks her to write him a poem. "I told him I didn't know how," Erwitt sighs. "I found out that he used to write poetry but had given up almost everything since his accident. He told me that when I go outside I should touch the world with my heart and not my hands. I said, 'See, you can still write poems. Why don't you just tell someone to write it down for you?' He got really sad and said, 'Oh I can't, I can't.'" As Erwitt is about to leave, one of the nurses comes up and hands her a poem Thomas has just dictated.

For the video teams, the day is like a play within a play: the subject, the still photographer recording the subject, the video crew chronicling the whole scene. The teams have their moments of the sublime and the surreal. Douglas Kirkland films a photographer covering a school on Kauai. A kid comes up and says, "Johnny really knows how to break." Kirkland doesn't know what that means. Break? Break what? Instantaneously, Johnny jumps straight up in the air, comes down on his head, and whirls around on his back in the seemingly effortless movements of break dancing.

Israeli photographer Alon Reininger is assigned to the military, with special attention to a bomb they'll be setting off for his benefit. A video team follows him. He's been heard to say, "I'd give anything to be at the beginning of the film." The bomb seems like a sure bet. Reininger is almost ready to shoot, when a deafening sound is heard. The military has let the bomb go a few minutes too soon. That evening, Hawaii's television viewers are amused as they watch the stoic face of the military officer in charge as he tries to explain to the assembled reporters and television crews why the bomb went off early.

Photographer Donna Ferrato and her daughter Fanny.

MAGGIE STEBER *courtesy Eastman Kodak*

Diego Goldberg of Argentina and Sebastiao Salgado of Brazil.

...courtesy Eastman Kodak

Photographer Dirck Halstead (left) is debriefed by *DITLOHA* assignment editor (and *Life* magazine writer) Curt Sanburn.

MAGGIE STEBER *courtesy Eastman Kodak*

NANCY HOLLENBECK

Travel Photographer of the Year Cliff Hollenbeck, with the tropical killer whales at Sealife Park.

The Day After

The photographers turn in their film and go through a wo-pronged debriefing process: first, to make captions or the book; later, to tell their stories to the video cameras for the documentary. Perhaps because of lack of leep, everyone gets lively, even silly. Many of the photographers have faraway smiles as they listen to others ecount their experiences. It is as if they all shared in ome wonderful ancient tribal ritual.

Douglas Kirkland, at the top of his career, is reduced to unning up and down between floors at the Sheraton, rying to capture photographers for videotape interviews efore they slip out of the building. Office discipline reaks down, and people who for months have been nodels of efficiency wander around with their eyes lazed over, asking, "Does anyone here know how to fix he Xerox machine? Where is the phone?" By the end of he debriefing period, a large garbage bag is filled with undreds of rolls of film. A few photographers run their ands through the bag, picking up handfuls of film and etting them tumble like gold in a treasure chest.

Hawaii itself has contributed to the cooperative spirit mong the photographers. Many of them were npressed with the openness and generosity of the Hawaiian people. "Hawaiians are probably the friendliest people in the world," says Pulitzer Prize winner Eddie dams. "I travel eleven months out of the year. Everyone lways asked me, 'Where is the most beautiful place ou've ever been?' Well, this is my first trip to Hawaii nd I think I've finally found the answer to that uestion."

You feel a tremendous warmth from people here," grees Jay Maisel, one of the world's top commercial hotographers. "I was overwhelmed by how nice everyne is. You know damn well that you'd be suspicious of his kind of warmth back in New York. But here it eems appropriate and genuine."

Michael Evans, President Reagan's personal photographer, spent the days leading up to December 2 finding individuals willing to pose for formal portraits on "The Day." "What I like about Hawaii is that people walk in and say 'hi' and it is like you are part of the family almost right away. It's totally different from the mainland.

That night the photographers celebrate at a luau. They continue to trade "war" stories. A Tahitian dancing group entertains. The photographers are polite enough. A few snicker and sneak peeks (and, of course, photos) of the dancing girls behind a bamboo screen, changing from coconut shells and grass skirts to batik wraps and flower headdresses. During the audience participation even the most reticent photographer is fair game. When *Time* magazine editor Arnold Drapkin gets in on the hula dancing, at least fifty people he's hired over the years crowd around—the infamous media hounds—pushing and shoving to get the best shot.

Tomorrow Drapkin and six other picture editors from leading publications and picture agencies will begin their jobs, taking approximately 64,800 photos and whittling them down to 400, maximum.

It is generally known in the international photojournalism community that no one can hula like *Time* magazine picture editor Arnold Drapkin.

RICK SMOLAN

Doubilet

The Hawaiian Islands are some of the most isolated islands in the world. For a fish caught in the great streams of the Pacific, the Hawaiian Islands are kind of a last gas station before oblivion.

You swim in and you see the edge of the crater, then you begin to sink down and the water turns from a light blue to a darker blue-black and almost to a blue-white. The inside of the crater was full of lemon butterfly fish. When you feed them they come around you in vast schools just like butterflies.... It's a kind of underwater studio—blue walls, a little bit of coral here and there, and unbelievably beautiful fish....

I poked my head in a hole. Two moray eels, one was in the background hiding behind the other... one of the eels came to the camera, kind of touched me, and touched the dome of the camera....

MAGGIE STEBER courtesy Eastman Kodak

The ***DITLOHA*** **Betacam documentary team (left to right): Stan Forman, Tibor Hirsch, David Burnett, Frank Beacham, Douglas Kirkland.**

DAVID BURNETT

The *Day in the Life of Hawaii* picture editors (left to right): John Durniak, Eliane Laffont, Howard Chapnick, Leslie Smolan and Arnold Drapkin. Kneeling in front: Robert Pledge and Woodfin Camp.

GREGORY HEISLER

All fifty of the *Day in the Life of Hawaii* photographers pose for Gregory Heisler shortly before leaving Honolulu on their assignments.

Epilogue

Cohen and Smolan each have their own thoughts about why the *Day in the Life* projects work. "We all get so caught up in our day-to-day assignments that most of us never have a chance to really reflect on what we are doing with our lives, with our photographs," Smolan says. "One of my goals with the *Day in the Life* projects is to give the people I admire—my personal heroes, the world's top photographers—a chance to catch their breath, to spend time with other photographers whom they admire and respect, to exchange ideas, and to apply their creativity to a unique place in a collaborative way."

"Photojournalism has to be the greatest form of delayed adolescence ever invented," says Cohen, who is known as "the zoo keeper" to the photographers. "These are people who never settle down and often never grow up, which is sometimes a problem if you are the one who has to handle their problems. But they also retain the good things about being young. They look at the world in a unique way, with an almost childlike curiosity. They don't seem to age the same way as other people. I guess I consider myself an honorary photojournalist. I've never been a working photographer but I identify very strongly with the group. I love working with photographers. I can't think of another group of people who are more interesting, exciting, or kind."

On the plane flying home, photographers Diego Goldberg and J. P. Laffont, from Argentina and France respectively, drink champagne and look at the photo album that J. P. has put together during the last week. It looks like anyone's family album of a trip—a photographer playing with her two-year-old during a slow moment, the photographers glumly trying to learn how to use their computers, silly poses of each member of the "family" with pithy autographs.

The photographers fly off to resume their normal lives. They're out there now, competing against each other for stories. They'll meet by accident in dark bars in Malaysia, on war-torn battlefields, in the mad crush of equipment and flesh surrounding a politician. For a few days on the *DITLOHA* project they have been able to get together on neutral ground, share secrets of the trade and again, just hang out as a family. At the height of confusion on "The Day," Smolan surveys the scene and says, "The bottom line is how to have fun and be creative at the same time. A three-ring circus is what this is all about."

And nothing captures this more than the photographers posing for their own silly, preposterous group portrait. One day after their briefings, those intrepid souls were told to go down to the beach and change into flamboyant pink Hawaiian shirts borrowed from the waiters at the nearby Royal Hawaiian Hotel. Thirty feet from shore, Gregory Heisler sits perched on a high, narrow scaffolding, waves lapping at the stilts. The photographers are instructed to wade out in the water up to their necks with their cameras held high in salute. There's a terrible moment of silence on Waikiki Beach. They all look at each other. No way!

"It was horrible," reminisces Heisler. "As soon as they got in front of the camera it was like they all had instant amnesia. They turned into John Travolta and the Chairman of the Board—complete prima donnas. These are the same guys who were full of bravado and war stories in the bar an hour before, and now it's 'I can't go in the water! I've photographed wars! Are you done yet? I've been shot at by bullets! I gotta go. You're taking too long. The light's gone. What's wrong? I'm cold, I'm tired, I'm hungry. Who is this guy?' " Then slowly they begin to wade in. For twenty-five minutes they stand in 75°F water, laughing and complaining and acting like an errant group of kindergartners on a class trip. They wade out. New York photographer Star Black, in wet white pants, becomes the butt of many a joke and tease. And, of course, days later Heisler is furious and upset at how the picture turned out and wants to do it over again. No way!

Lisa See
Publishers Weekly

Photographers' Biographies

Abbas Iran
A member of the prestigious Magnum Agency, Abbas has covered Africa, the Middle East and Asia for the past ten years and most recently completed a one-year project photographing Mexico. He won the first Olivier Rebbot Award.

Saigon 1969

Eddie Adams USA
Adams has received more than 400 awards for his photographic work in the U.S. and overseas, including the 1969 Pulitzer Prize for News Photography and, in 1975, the National Press Photographers Association award for Magazine Photographer of the Year. Adams has been a contract photographer for both *Time* magazine and the Associated Press.

eru 1981

William Albert Allard USA
A former staff photographer for *National Geographic* magazine, Allard's work has also appeared in *Life, Sports Illustrated* and *GEO.* His award-winning study of cowboy life in the American West, *Vanishing Breed,* was published by the New York Graphic Society in 1982. In 1983, he received the American Society of Magazine Photographers' Outstanding Achievement Award.

F. Bentley USA
Bentley began his photojournalism career in Hawaii as staff photographer for the now-defunct *Sunbums* tabloid. Since 1976, he has been a contributor to *Newsweek, The New York Times, USA Today* and *Time.* Most recently, Bentley was *Time*'s man on the John Glenn presidential campaign.

Star Black USA
A former staff photographer with UPI, Black's work has appeared in books, major newspapers, magazines, and travel guides. In 1982, her work in the book *Texas Boots,* published by Viking, was nominated for a National Book Award in the category "Illustration of Art Collectibles." Black was born and raised in Hawaii and now lives in New York.

David Burnett USA
Burnett's extensive coverage of world events for the world's leading news and picture magazines has been recognized with numerous awards including the Overseas Press Club's Robert Capa Gold Medal, a grand prize in the World Press Photo Competition and the Best Photographic Reporting from Abroad award from the Overseas Press Club of America. Burnett is a founding member of Contact Press Images, and one of the five cameramen who worked on the *DITLOHA* video documentary.

RENE BURRI
A Day in the Life of Australia 1981

Rene Burri Switzerland
Burri is an accomplished film maker and a regular contributor to major magazines in the U.S. and Europe, including *Life, Stern* and the London Sunday *Times.* Well-known for his book *The Germans,* published in 1962, Burri is at work on another collection of photographs drawn from a major exhibition, "Rene Burri—One World," held in Zurich in 1983. Burri is a member of the Magnum Agency.

Aaron Chang USA
Since 1979, Chang has been senior staff photographer for *Surfing* magazine. In 1982 he received the American Society of Magazine Photographers' Award of Excellence and was named one of the five best sports photographers in the U.S. by *American Photographer* magazine. His work has also appeared in *Stern,* French *Vogue* and *Gentlemen's Quarterly.*

Paul Chesley USA
A free-lance photographer based in Aspen, Colorado, Chesley is a regular contributor to the *National Geographic, GEO, Time* and other publications. Solo exhibitions of his work have been held in the U.S. and Japan, including a 1984 show at the Academy of Arts in Honolulu.

Jerry Chong USA
During his years as staff photographer for the *Honolulu Advertiser,* Chong won numerous photojournalism awards. In 1959, *Life* magazine cited his coverage of the volcanic eruptions at Kilauea with the prestigious Photo of the Year award. Now one of Hawaii's leading commercial photographers, Chong's work is included in the collection of the Metropolitan Museum of Art, New York.

Rich Clarkson USA
Clarkson is assistant managing editor of the *Denver Post* and the former picture editor of the *Topeka Capital-Journal.* He most recently covered the Olympic Games in Los Angeles for *Sports Illustrated,* his fifth summer Olympics assignment. As a lecturer, contributor, editor and *eminence gris* of American photography, Clarkson has worked with universities, professional associations and newspapers. His work has appeared in *Time, Life* and the *Saturday Evening Post.*

JODI COBB
A Day in the Life of Australia 1981

Jodi Cobb USA
A staff photographer for *National Geographic,* Cobb's most recent stories include coverage of London, Jerusalem and Jordan. Her photos from an eight-thousand-mile trip across China in 1981 were published in the Society's book, *Journey Into China.* She was one of the subjects of a recent PBS documentary entitled "On Assignment."

Bob Davis Australia
Based in Hong Kong, Davis travels extensively for editorial, advertising and corporate photo assignments. He has won several CLIO awards for his corporate photography. A collection of his black-and-white photographs was published in the book *Faces of Japan.* In 1979 Davis formed Hong Kong's first picture agency, The Stock House.

ARNAUD DE WILDENBERG
A Day in the Life of Australia 1981

Arnaud De Wildenberg France
De Wildenberg is best known for his coverage of the Afghanistan crisis and Iranian and Cambodian refugees. He won the *Paris-Match* contest for the best news report in 1980 for his work in Uganda and an award from the World Press Photo Foundation for his coverage of Lech Walesa in Poland. His photograph of a diver appeared on the cover of *A Day in the Life of Australia.*

David Doubilet USA
Doubilet is considered to be the world's leading underwater photographer. Over twenty of his underwater photo stories have appeared in the *National Geographic.* He has won numerous prizes for his specialized photography, including the prestigious SARA Prize, an Italian award for underwater photography.

DAN DRY
A Day in the Life of Australia 1981

Dan Dry USA
Based in Kentucky, Dry is a free-lance photographer for *National Geographic* and other domestic and foreign publications. His newspaper work was recognized by the National Press Photographers Association when he was named National Newspaper Photographer of the Year in 1981.

Elliott Erwitt USA
One of America's leading photographers and a member of Magnum Photos, Erwitt's work has appeared in the world's major magazines over the last 25 years. Erwitt has also become a well-known film maker, producing independent documentaries and a series of films for Home Box Office. Erwitt's books include *Photographs and Anti-Photographs, Son of Bitch, Observations on American Architecture* and *Recent Developments.*

Jennifer Erwitt USA
Jennifer Erwitt served as production manager for the *DITLOHA* project. Her photographs have appeared in the New York *Daily News* and *Frets* magazine. She is the founding member of Feline Productions.

Michael Evans Canada
Evans is the personal photographer to President Reagan. Prior to reaching that special vantage point, Evans covered Reagan's 1976 nomination campaign and 1980 election as a contract photographer for *Time* magazine.

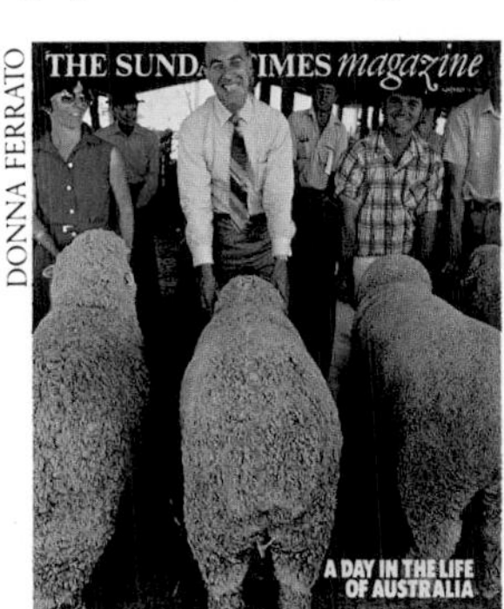

DONNA FERRATO

Donna Ferrato USA
Ferrato's work has appeared in *Life, Fortune, Newsweek, The New York Times, Bunte* and Japanese *Playboy.* Ferrato's photographs often capture the humorous or bizarre side of human behavior. Ferrato is the mother of Fanny Ferrato.

Dana Fineman USA
Fineman studied photography at the Art Center College of Design in Pasadena and worked for several years as an assistant to well-known celebrity photographer Douglas Kirkland. Fineman's work appears frequently in *People* magazine, *American Health* and *American Photographer.* Based in Los Angeles, Fineman is associated with Sygma Photos.

FRANK FOURNIER

Lebanon 1983

Frank Fournier France
Fournier's work has appeared in a broad array of magazines and journals, including *Paris-Match, Forbes, Le Figaro, Time* and *The New York Times Magazine.* In 1983 he photographed major stories on the Pope's travels in Europe and Central America, the dancer Baryshnikov and the conflict in Lebanon. He is a member of Contact Press Images.

J. Carl Ganter USA
The youngest member of the *DITLOHA* team, Ganter is a sophomore at Northwestern University. He managed to get both U.S. Secret Service press credentials and a membership in the elite Nikon Professional Services organization before he was 15. His work has appeared in the *Detroit News* and the Dutch magazine *Der Tijd.*

Sam Garcia USA
Formerly an Atlanta-based freelance photographer, Garcia is field manager for Nikon Technical and Professional Services, working out of New York. While working for Nikon he has covered NASA space launches, the Kentucky Derby, the Indianapolis 500 and the Summer Olympic Games in Los Angeles.

Wilbur E. Garrett USA
The editor of *National Geographic* magazine, Garrett is also a working photographer. His byline for photography and text has appeared in *National Geographic* more than 29 times. Among his awards and honors, Garrett has received the Newhouse Citation from Syracuse University, the Distinguished Service in Journalism award from the University of Missouri, and Magazine Photographer of the Year from the National Press Photographers Association.

DIEGO GOLDBERG

West Germany 1979

Diego Goldberg Argentina
After beginning his photojournalism career in Latin America as a correspondent for Camera Press, Goldberg moved to the Paris office in 1977, and then to New York in 1980. Now with the Sygma Photo Agency, his work has been featured in major magazines throughout the world.

Robert B. Goodman USA
A resident of Hawaii, Goodman is known both locally and internationally for his two landmark photo books, *The Australians* and *The Hawaiians.* Goodman began his career as a staff photographer at *National Geographic* magazine.

Rita Gormley USA
An avid photographer, Gormley is the editor of *Aloha* magazine, a picture magazine about Hawaii that is distributed nationally.

Arthur Grace USA
Grace's most recent work includes coverage of the Pope's trip to Poland, the 1983 America's Cup races and a soon-to-be-published book of personal photographs. His photos have appeared in *Time, Life, Look, Newsweek,* the London Sunday *Times, Paris-Match* and *Bunte.* Grace is associated with the Sygma Photo Agency.

DIRCK HALSTEAD

Dirck Halstead USA
Halstead has been a working photographer for more than 20 years, covering world news events for UPI and, more recently, as a contract photographer for *Time* magazine. Honored with many professional awards, Halstead also claims the distinction of shooting more *Time* covers than any other individual photographer in the magazine's history. His running count: 33.

DAVID ALAN HARVEY

David Alan Harvey Canada
Harvey's assignments during 10 years as staff photographer for the *National Geographic* include Honduras, Kampuchea, the Arctic, Spain and Malaysia. In 1978 he was chosen Magazine Photographer of the Year by the National Press Photographers Association.

GREGORY HEISLER

A Day in the Life of Australia 1981

Gregory David Heisler USA
Heisler's photographs have been published in such magazines as *Life, GEO, Fortune, Connoisseur* and *Time.* He produced the last two performance books of the American Ballet Theater and intends to do more fashion photography in the near future.

Cliff Hollenbeck USA
Hollenbeck, based in Seattle, specializes in travel and advertising photography and was named Travel Photographer of the Year in 1983. His work has been published by the *National Geographic, Travel & Leisure, Sunset* and other major magazines.

Ron Jett USA
Jett, a staff photographer for the *Honolulu Advertiser,* has completed special assignments for *Time, Newsweek, Fortune* and *U.S. News & World Report.* Jett began his photo career at the *Tampa Tribune* and the *Sarasota Journal* in Florida before moving to Hawaii in 1976.

Shelly Katz USA
At the age of 12, Katz had his first picture published in the New York *Daily News.* Based in Dallas since 1965, Katz has photographed everything from fast-breaking news to glamour and sports for most of the leading international magazines and as a contract photographer for *Time* magazine. Katz is represented by the Black Star Photo Agency.

Douglas Kirkland Canada
Kirkland is one of the world's best known glamour and personality photographers. Twenty-three years in the business include camera work with Marilyn Monroe, Judy Garland, Barbra Streisand and Christie Brinkley. Based in Los Angeles, he was one of the founding members of Contact Press Images. Kirkland was responsible for producing the *DITLOHA* video documentary.

Kent J. Kobersteen USA
Before joining the *National Geographic* as illustrations editor in 1983, Kobersteen was staff photographer and picture editor at the Minneapolis *Tribune,* a job which took him to over 20 countries, primarily in Africa, the Middle East and Asia. He has won several awards from the Overseas Press Club of America as well as the 1982 World Hunger Media Award for Photography.

Jean-Pierre Laffont France
Laffont attended the prestigious School of Graphic Arts in Vevey, Switzerland prior to serving in the French army in Algeria in the early 1960s. He has served as a U.S. correspondent for Reporters Associates and the Gamma Photo Agency. Since 1973 he has been a partner of the Sygma Photo Agency based in New York. His work appears in the world's leading news magazines.

Wayne A. Levin USA
Levin began his career as assistant to well-known Honolulu photographer Robert Wenkham. He received his MFA from Pratt Institute, New York, in 1982 and now teaches photography at the University of Hawaii. Exhibitions of his work have been held in New York, Los Angeles, San Francisco and at the Academy of Arts in Honolulu.

JOHN LOENGARD

Bill Cosby 1969

John Loengard USA
Loengard originated the *Day in the Life* concept when he produced "One Day In The Life of America" as a *Life* magazine Special Report in 1974. A staff photographer for *Life* in the 1960s, Loengard went on to become the first picture editor at *People.* Instrumental in the revival of *Life* in 1978, he currently serves as the magazine's picture editor.

GERD LUDWIG

Saudi Arabia 197

Gerd Ludwig West Germany
A founding member of VISUM Photographic Agency in Hamburg, Ludwig is a regular contributor to *GEO, Life, Zeit-Magazin, Stern, Fortune* and other magazines. He is a member of Deutsche Gesellschaft für Photographie (German Photographic Society) and the Art Directors Club of Germany.

Leonard Lueras USA
Lueras moved to Hawaii from Southern California in 1963. Since then, he has become a leading editor/publisher/writer of books and articles on Pacific-area subjects, including the best-selling *Insight Guide to Hawaii,* which he produced and edited. Lueras' most recent writing effort, *Surfing: The Ultimate Pleasure,* was published by Emphasis International and distributed in the U.S. by Workman Publishing of New York.

Portugal 1972

Jay Maisel USA
Maisel's work appears regularly in magazines, advertisements and corporate publications. His color prints are included in numerous corporate and private collections. He received the Outstanding Achievement in Photography Award from the American Society of Magazine Photographers in 1978 and the Newhouse Citation from Syracuse University in 1979. In 1982, he was a participant in the Nikon "Photographer's Eye" interview series.

Stephanie Maze USA
Born in New York and raised in Germany, Maze spent six years as a staff photographer for the *San Francisco Chronicle*. She covered the Montreal, Moscow and Los Angeles Olympic Games for the Associated Press and is now a free-lance photographer kept busy, for the most part, by assignments from the *National Geographic*.

abra McCracken USA
A free-lance photographer now based in Anchorage, Alaska, McCracken was born and raised in Hawaii. She is a graduate of Kamehameha School and the University of Hawaii. Her work has appeared in National Geographic Society special publications and other magazines.

Robin Moyer USA
Moyer's coverage of the conflict in Lebanon was recognized with two prestigious awards in 1983: the Press Photo of the Year Award in the World Press Photo Competition; and a Robert Capa Gold Medal citation from the Overseas Press Club of America. Represented by the Gamma-Liaison Photo Agency, his work appears in *Time, Newsweek, GEO, Smithsonian* and other magazines.

Matthew Naythons USA
A working photojournalist and physician, Naythons has spent most of his career alternating photo coverage of world events with emergency room duty in San Francisco. In 1979 he founded an emergency medical team to care for Cambodian and Thai refugees. His photographic work appears in major magazines including *Stern*, the London Sunday *Times, Newsweek* and *Time*.

Kazuyoshi Nomachi Japan
Japanese photographer Nomachi began free-lancing in 1971. He has become known around the world for his two books *The Sahara* and *The Sinai*, which were published in five languages. His work on the Nile has appeared in *Life, Stern, Figaro* and *Oggi*. In early 1984 he won the Ken Damon Prize for Books.

MICHAEL O'BRIEN

A Day in the Life of Australia 1981

Michael O'Brien USA
A native of Memphis, O'Brien began his career at the *Miami News*, where his work was recognized with two Robert F. Kennedy Journalism Awards for Outstanding Coverage of the Disadvantaged. His work now appears frequently in *Life, GEO* and other magazines.

DENNIS ODA

Hawaii 1983

Dennis Oda USA
Originally from the Pacific Northwest, Oda came to Hawaii to study zoology in a graduate program at the University of Hawaii. Five years ago, he became a staff photographer at the *Honolulu Star-Bulletin*.

Gordon Parks USA
Parks was one of *Life* magazine's foremost photographers in the 1960s. He later went on to write several books including *The Learning Tree*, compose several musical pieces, and direct a number of Hollywood films (*Shaft*). Parks directed the *Day in the Life of Hawaii* video documentary and was also a still photographer on the project.

Eli Reed USA
Reed is a veteran of the *Middletown* (N.Y.) *Record* and the *Detroit News*. For the *San Francisco Chronicle*, he has covered urban poverty and the conflicts in Central America and Lebanon. In 1982, he was granted a prestigious Nieman Fellowship at Harvard University. Reed is associated with the Magnum Photo Agency.

Alon Reininger Israel
Upheavals in Nicaragua and El Salvador, developments in Honduras, the AIDS epidemic, the development of the Cruise and Pershing II missiles and cocaine smuggling in Florida are among Reininger's recent stories for the world's leading magazines. He is a founding member of Contact Press Images.

Ken Sakamoto Canada
Sakamoto has photographed the Royal Family at Windsor Castle and walrus hunts in the Arctic. His work has appeared in several Canadian newspapers, *Time, Newsweek, Life, Sports Illustrated* and other magazines in Europe, Japan and South America. He is currently a staff photographer for the *Honolulu Star-Bulletin* and is associated with Black Star Photo Agency.

Sebastiao Salgado Brazil
Associated with the Magnum Photo Agency, Salgado's work has been seen in *Time, Paris-Match, Stern*, the London Sunday *Times* and *Fortune*. His ongoing study of the indigenous peoples of Latin America was recognized with the Eugene Smith Award in 1982.

FRANK SALMOIRAGHI

Hawaii 1982

Frank Salmoiraghi USA
Salmoiraghi has lived and photographed in Hawaii since 1968. His work has been published and exhibited frequently in Honolulu and on the mainland. An occasional college-level teacher, he is represented by the APA Photo Agency in Singapore and by The Art Loft and Gallery EAS in Honolulu.

Allan Seiden USA
A travel writer/photographer specializing in adventure, history and outdoor subjects, Seiden is a contributor to several leading travel magazines and newspapers. He travels frequently to South America, the South Pacific and Asia from his home base in Honolulu.

Michael Shayegani Iran
Shayegani came to the U.S. from Iran in 1969 and attended Drexel University. After borrowing his father's Rolloflex at the age of 14, he developed an interest in photography and, several years later, moved to Los Angeles to begin free-lancing. Since 1979 he has worked as an assistant to glamour photographer Douglas Kirkland.

RICK SMOLAN

South Korea 1978

Rick Smolan USA
Director of the *DITLOHA* project, Smolan is also responsible for the book *A Day In the Life of Australia*, published in 1981. Previous to these extravaganzas, he was a full-time photojournalist whose work appeared in *Life, Fortune, Time, Newsweek, The New York Times, National Geographic* and other journals. In 1983 Smolan was awarded the New York Art Directors Club Gold Medal Award. He is one of the founders of the PHOTO-1 computer communications network.

Shomei Tomatsu Japan
In 1976 Tomatsu received the Japanese Education Minister's Art Encouragement Award. In 1981, his exhibition "The World of Shomei Tomatsu" was displayed in Japan's major cities.

Neal Ulevich USA
Ulevich won the Pulitzer Prize for News Photography in 1977 during his stint as Southeast Asia correspondent for the Associated Press. On December 3, 1983, a day after his assignment with the Hilo and Honolulu Police Departments for *A Day In The Life of Hawaii*, Ulevich flew to Beijing to become AP's man in mainland China.

Mark S. Wexler USA
A free-lance photographer based in New York, Wexler has worked for *Time, Newsweek, Fortune, The New York Times* and *Smithsonian*. His major stories include robotics and coverage of Underwriters Laboratories.

Steve Wilkings USA
Wilkings, a California native, established himself as a commercial photographer in Honolulu in the early 1970s. Best known for his wind-surfing and surfing photographs, Wilkings has had his work published in *Playboy, Penthouse, Time, Yachting, Sail, Surfing* and *Wind Surf*.

David Yamada USA
David Yamada has covered nearly every major news event in Hawaii over the past 15 years as staff photographer for the *Honolulu Advertiser*. His pictures have appeared in *Time, Newsweek, U.S. News & World Report* and a number of European and Asian journals.

Staff Members

The Book Project

Produced and Directed by:
Rick Smolan and
David Cohen

Manager
Bill Peabody

Logistics Coordinator
Anne Edmonson

Assignment Editor
J. Curtis Sanburn

Associate Assignment Editor
Larry Levin

Caption and Debriefing Coordinator
Sean Callahan
American Photographer Magazine

Production Coordinator
Jennifer Erwitt

Production Assistant
Kai Sanburn

Administrative Assistants
Lisa Matsukawa (Honolulu)
Margot Knight (New York)

Traffic Manager
Renata Haarhoff
Time Inc.

Public Relations Consultants
Sharon Weiner and
Sheila Donnelly
Stryker Weiner Associates

Stress Management
Tanya Bova

Project Logo Design
Laura Sanburn

Legal Advisor
F. Richard Pappas
Paul, Weiss, Rifkind, Wharton & Garrison

Business Advisor
Jeffrey Epstein
The Washington Post Company

Insurance Advisor
John Beck
Beck-York Associates

Chief Picture Editor
Arnold Drapkin
Time Magazine

Picture Editors
G. Woodfin Camp
Woodfin Camp & Associates
Howard Chapnick
Black Star Publishing
John Durniak
The New York Times
Eliane Laffont
Sygma Photos
Robert Pledge
Contact Press Images

Designer
Leslie Smolan
Gottschalk & Ash Int'l

Design Assistants
Diane Lemasters
Kathy Herlihy
Richard Rew
Judith Rew
Cindy Steinberg
Beverly McLean

Captions
J. Curtis Sanburn

Workman Publishing
Peter Workman
Publisher
Carolan Workman
Director, Subsidiary Rights
Sally Kovalchick
Editor-in-Chief
Paul Hanson
Art Director
Wayne Kirn
Production Manager
Jennifer Rogers
Publicity Director
Mary Wilkinson
Copy Editor

The Documentary

Executive Producers
David Cohen and
Rick Smolan

Producer
Douglas Kirkland

Director
Gordon Parks

Executive in Charge of Production
Shep Morgan

Assistant Producer
J. Curtis Sanburn

Technical Advisor
Larry Thorpe
The Sony Corporation of America

Production Coordinator
Eric Weyenberg

Videographers
Frank Beacham
David Burnett
Stan Foreman
Tibor Hirsch
Douglas Kirkland

Sound
Mike Michaels

Production Assistants
Cliff Watson
Robin Stephens
Vicki Keith

Conference on Photojournalism

Coordinator
Bill Peabody

From the East-West Center
Jim McMann
Diane Dods
Wesley Park
Greg Knudsen

Agents

France
Annie Boulat, Cosmos
56 Boulevard de la Tour Maubourg
75007 Paris
Phone 705 4429, Telex 203085

Germany
Marita Kankowski, Focus
Schlueterstrasse 6
2000 Hamburg 13
Phone 44 3769, Telex 2164242

Italy
Grazia Neri
Via Senato 18
20121 Milano
Phone 79 9275, Telex 312575

Japan
Bob Kirschenbaum
Pacific Press
CPO 2051, Tokyo
Phone 264 3821, Telex 26206

United Kingdom
Terry Le Goubin
Colorific Photo Library
Gilray House, Gloucester Terrace, London W2
Phone (01) 723 5031 or 402 9595

United States
Woodfin Camp & Associates
415 Madison Avenue
New York, NY 10017
Phone (212) 750 1020
Telex 428788

Advisors, Contributors and Consultants

Shelly Katz

Paul Addison
Bob Agres
Danita Aiu
Reverend Akaka
Charlene Aldinger
Lancaster Allen
Emmett Aluli
Dawn Amano
David Ames
Juan Aquinde
Tom Araki
Angel Aranio
Gov. and Mrs.
George Ariyoshi
Henry Ariyoshi
Phil Arnone
Geraldine Asmus
William Aull
John Beck
Ruth Ann Becker
John Bellinger
Cobey Black
Roy & Jackie Blackshear
Glen Blinde
Del Borer
Ann Boresguard
Jeanne Bowman
Patricia Bowman
David Boynton
Cheryl Boynton
Manfred Braig
Steve Brazil
Carl Bredhoff
John Breglio
Wendy Brennan
Christiana Breustedt
Kenny Brown
Corky Bryan
Buck Buchwach
Edward Burns
Robert Burns
Susan Burns
ane and Peter Cambouris
Vance Cannon
im Cardin
Anna Cariagi
Don Carroll
im Cartlin
Wayne Carvalho
Edward Case
aul Cassiday
ill Chang Jr.
George Chaplin
en Char
ylvia Chase
athy Chin
abby Choy
ıdy Ann Christensen
ohn Christiansen
aniel S. Cohen
annah Cohen
Norman Cohen
arles B. Cooper
uernsey Curren
Tom Daniels
Alberta Dejetly
Kila DeMello
Walter Dods
Jim Domke
Brendan Donnelly
Cornelius Downs
Larry Doyle
Gene Driskell
Gayle Driskell
Natasha Driskell
Reverend Du Teil
Diane Duffy
Francine Duncan
Kelen Dunford
John Dvorak
Mike Einstein
George Ellis
Mickey Endo
Sue Epstein
Mary Evangelista
John Fairbank
Marci Farias
Diane Ferry
Kamala Rose Fontaine
Judith S. Fox
Marlene Freedman
Hans Friedrichs
Jocelyn Fujii
Dennis Fujii
David Fujimoto
Tex Fuller
Dr. John B. Garver, Jr.
Jim Gary
Janice Glickson
Jim Good
Marvin Goodhue
Milton Goto
Sybil Grace
Marcia Graham
Peter Greenberg
Clancy Greff
Nui Gurtner
Thomas Gurtner
Jack Gushiken
Grace Guslander
Charlotte Hamada
Jo Ann Hamilton
Babes Hanchett
Neil Hannah
Harry Hasegawa
Jan Hayashi
Michael Henderson
Gordan Hentschel
Mary Hernlund
Arnold Higa
Rex Higa
Don Hillis
John Hirashima
Saj Ho
Melvin Ho
Robert Holden
Randy Holt
Aka Hodgins
Karen Hong
Stanley Hong
Linda Howe
David Hudson
Harry Hueu
B. J. Hughes
Julia Hunt
David Hunter
Chris Ikeda
Maizie Ishimaru
Vern Iuppa
Larry Iyomasa
Ron Jacobs
Larry Johnson
Fred Johnson
Roger Jones
Russ Jones
Gerry Jordan
Elisa Josephsohn
Mary Kaczmarik
Elizabeth Kaiser
Mitsuo Kajiwara
Michael Kakesako
Charmane Kamaka
Dorothea Kanenaka
Esther Kau
Harry Kauhane
Julia Kaupu
Bee Kaya
Jerry Keir
Kent Keith
Joel Kennedy
Gloria Kern
Dori Kim
Val Kim-Friar
Benita Kostic
Tom Kreiger
Vereena Kulenkampff
Don Kuyper
Chapman Lam
Cindy Lawrence
Doug Lee
Eric LeFauvre
Ron Leong
Jack Lewin
Terri Liberman
Carl Lindquist
Alice Lloyd
Rosalind Loomis
Jim Luckey
Kay Lund
Tiny Malaikini
Irwin Maltzman
Alfred Mandell
John Markoff
Chuck Marshall
Esther Martinez
Ray Massey
Mayor Herbert Matayoshi
Maryanne May
Douglas MacArthur
Dodie MacArthur
Betty McCart
Helen McCord
Cmdr. Joseph McGrath
Roderick McPhee
Pat Megson
Barbara Meheula
Maurice Meyers
Blaine Michioka
Barbara Mills
Howard Mimaki
Tony Mina
Phillip Moffitt
Pinkie Mookini
Gary Moore
John R. Morgan
Daniel Moriarty
Bessie Morita
Pat Morosic
F. L. Morris
Marsha Morrison
Karen Murphy
Joan Naguwa
Sheryl Neuman
Karen Newton
George Niitani
Don Nixon
Chuck Novak
John O'Brien
Bob O'Conner
Randie O'Shaunessey
Dan O'Shea
Pat Oakes
Allen Okimoto
Nora Okumura
Alice Okuna
Adam Osborne
George Ota
Don Over
Josie Over
Tai Over
Bob Ozaki
Ted Paiva
Bill Pakela
Jerry Panzo
Jim Parker
Margy Parker
Nick Pechin
Ali Peed
Joseph Pelletier
Verna Perkins
Gabe Perle
Linda Perreira
Gregg Perry
Anna Perry-Fiske
Bob Peters
Robert Pfeiffer
Jeff Phillips
Dick Post
Bart Potter
Dudley Pratt
Dick Pultz
Carol Putnam
Pat Reid
Bill Rhodes
Mark Richards
Monty Richards
Jim Richardson
Joseph Ridder
Walter Ritte
Sheila Roback
Fred Robinson
Lori Robinson
Ronn Ronck
Mark Rublee
Richard Ruff
Tom Ryder
Lori Sablas
Edward Sakata
Will Sanburn
Marta Sanburn
Betsy Sandstrom
Carol Saner
Ray Sasaki, Jr.
Jan-Michel Sawyer
Amy Schiffman
Elaine Scott
Lisa See
Jan Selland
Anne Shackelford
Billie Shaddix
Alex Shapiro
Bruce Shirley
Momi Shoemaker
Don Sholly
Katie Simpson
Andrea Simpson
Richard Smart
William W. Smith
Kit Smith
Fred Smith
Ned Smith
Gloria Smolan
Marvin Smolan
Sandy Smolan
Pilipo Solatorio & Family
Laura Spain
Mary Spain
Bob Springer
Ron Stegall
Robin Stephens
Cori Stockman
Jim Stockton
Doc Stryker
Rex Stucky
Peter Suyat
Manuel Sylvester
Calvin Takeda
Ray Tanaka
Ed Tanji
Hannibal Tavares
Jan TenBruggencate
Carrie Teraoka
Glenn Teves
Andrew Thomson
Art Tokin
Sgt. Torres
Thurston Twigg-Smith
John Urauchi
Della Van Heyst
Jean Vile
Ron Villegas
Larry Vogel
Jennifer Walker
Suzie Waltjen
Richard Waltjen
Jeff Watanabe
J. D. Watumull
Gulab & Indru Watumull
David Karl Wendlinger
Robert Wernett
Lael Weyenberg
Terry White
Betty White
Mele White Pochereva
Sila Williams
Dr. Henry Wong
Michelle Wong
Connie Wright
Mr. and Mrs. Harlow Wright
Jeanne Yagi
Rodney Yamaguchi
Takashi Yamashita
Burt Yoneshige
Wes Young
Rick Zwern

Mahalo to the people of Hawaii

Kazuyoshi Nomachi

Every once in a while, an idea comes along that seems to capture the fancy of everyone it touches. *A Day in the Life of Hawaii* began in Honolulu as a young woman's daydream and ended with the book you are now holding in your hands. This book seems to have willed itself into existence against all odds and obstacles. In a world of people with good intentions and projects which fall by the wayside, *A Day in the Life of Hawaii* proves that nothing is impossible if you believe in it strongly enough.

We are grateful to the fifty photographers who flew to Hawaii from all over the globe to apply their rare and prodigious skills with devotion, to the hundreds who photographed alongside the professionals, to the business community of Hawaii, which contributed generously, and to the more than five hundred individuals who participated in the final production. This book is a tribute to each of you and to Hawaii's belief in itself.

Project Sponsors

Underwriters
First Hawaiian Bank
Duty Free Shoppers
Matson Navigation, a division of Alexander & Baldwin, Inc.
Hawaiian Telephone
Pacific Resources, Inc.
Hawaii Visitors Bureau
Department of Planning and Economic Development

Subsidizers
The Honolulu Advertiser
Hawaiian Trust Company, Ltd.
Hawaiian Electric Company
Oceanic Cable Vision

Sponsors
Aloha Airlines
Coopers & Lybrand
Holiday Rent-a-Car System, Hawaii
Sony Corporation of America
Stryker Weiner Associates
The Westin Ilikai
Wang Laboratories

Major Sponsors
United Airlines
Sheraton Hotels of the Pacific
Eastman Kodak Company

Contributors
Apple Computer
Avis Rental Cars
Beachcomber Hotel
Central Pacific Divers
Emphasis, Inc.
Estate of James Campbell
General Videotex Corporation
The Kaanapali Beach Resort
Living Videotex Corporation
Mauna Loa Macadamia Nuts
Memory Lane Computers
Menehune Helicopters
NASA
Nikon Professional Services
Office Things, Inc.
Radio Shack
South Sea Helicopter
The Copy Center
The Mauna Lani Bay Hotel
The Mauna Lani Resort
The National Geographic Soc
The Photoplant
The Waiohai Resort
World Airways
Windjammer Cruises